Pitch Only

Bass Clef

Pitch Only – Bass Clef by Nathan Petitpas,
published by Dots and Beams, Toronto, Ontario, Canada.

©2020 Nathan Petitpas, Dots and Beams. All rights reserved.

No portion of this book may be copied or redistributed
without the permission of the publisher

ISBN 978-1-9992913-4-1

www.DotsandBeams.com

Contents

Introductions:

    About Dots and Beams..1

    About the Author..1

    Preface: How To Use This Book...2

Exercises:

    Chapter 1: On the Staff – Diatonic..3

    Chapter 2: On the Staff – Chromatic..11

    Chapter 3: Above the Staff – Diatonic..21

    Chapter 4: Above the Staff – Chromatic...34

    Chapter 5: Below the Staff – Diatonic..47

    Chapter 6: Below the Staff – Chromatic...60

    Chapter 7: On and Above the Staff – Diatonic...73

    Chapter 8: On and Above the Staff – Chromatic..86

    Chapter 9: On and Below the Staff – Diatonic...99

    Chapter 10: On and Below the Staff – Chromatic...112

About Dots and Beams

Have you ever created a musical exercise, for yourself or for a student, that would have been much more effective if you could just find a few pages of a certain type of reading material? Perhaps you're a drummer looking for pages of rhythms for developing your timing or coordination. Or maybe you're a pianist looking for melodic reading material to play in your right hand to help develop coordination with a difficult ostinato or bass line. Perhaps you're an experienced musician learning a second instrument; you may feel you would benefit from pages of random notes on a staff to help you become familiar with your new instrument. Or maybe you'd like to mix up your scale practice by playing your scales in unpredictable rhythms rather than the patterns you have been using for years. Maybe you've always played guitar by ear and have lately been wanting to learn to read music; you might want something graduated and systematic to read to help you learn the elements of musical notation but you don't want to play nursery rhymes.

Dots and Beams was created to provide a wide variety of reading materials for musicians at all skill levels and for all instruments.

My approach to creating reading material is slightly different from other approaches I've seen. Many other sight-reading books provide a series of musical compositions for use in practising sight-reading. Rather than provide books of compositions, my approach is to break down the language of musical notation into its rhythmic and melodic components and introduce these components to the user in a systematic way.

These pages of notes and rhythms are not intended to be seen as compositions: they do not follow any particular harmonic or melodic structure and the melodies they contain are not repetitive or memorable. They are exercises in which the complexity of the written language of music gradually increases in order to strengthen the user's ability to process the raw data of musical notation. While the Dots and Beams books are an excellent resource to help improve your sight-reading, their unique construction ensures that the additional uses for these books are as varied and individual as the musicians using them.

Each book in the Dots and Beams collection focuses on a specific element of musical notation. This ensures that you always have the perfect reading material for any exercise so that you can isolate the specific areas in your playing that you feel you need to work on. These books offer very little in the way of explanation and descriptions in an effort to provide as much note-reading material as possible. This is not so much a method book as it is a tool to help make practice more focused and effective.

My hope is that this collection will be one that you will revisit year after year as you find newer, more creative, and more challenging ways to use the materials to push your playing, and your students' playing, to new levels.

About the Author

Nathan Petitpas is a percussionist living in Toronto, Ontario, Canada. He works predominantly as a freelancer in the Ontario orchestral scene as well as the Toronto contemporary music scene. He teaches drum set, percussion, music theory, and general music classes in a variety of programs across Toronto. Nathan holds a Master of Music degree from the University of Toronto and a Bachelor of Music degree from Acadia University, both in percussion performance.

Preface: How To Use This Book

This book provides its user with a series of notes on a bass staff with no rhythm values and no meter. Chapters are organized by the placement of the notes relative to the staff; on the staff, above the staff, below the staff, on and above the staff, and on and below the staff. For each pitch range there is one chapter with no accidentals and one chapter with accidentals. All exercises have a space at the beginning of each staff to write in a key signature, allowing each exercise to be read in all keys and used in many ways.

The aim with this book is to allow the user to focus specifically on exercises centred around pitch without the distraction of rhythmic values or time signatures. This can begin with the practice of sight-reading but can expand to include many other learning goals.

The diatonic sets contain notes with no accidentals or key signature. These collections can be read as written, using only natural notes, or in any of the 15 key signatures from 7 flats to 7 sharps.

Chromatic collections include sharp and flat notes as well as natural ones. The later exercises in these chapters increase the difficulty by including B♯, C♭, E♯, and F♭.

Ledger line chapters start with the first ledger line and gradually expand away from the staff. Exercises above and below the staff extend to the space just beyond the fourth ledger line.

The random nature of the notes in these exercises is intentional; it forces the user to pay attention to each note and makes the exercises very difficult to memorize, ensuring that they will still present a challenge even after multiple readings.

It's important when sight-reading to cycle through the exercises quickly rather than dwelling on a single exercise for a long time. This will ensure that you're strengthening your ability to read the notes rather than just memorizing the exercises.

Some suggestions for how to use this book include:

- Gain comfort reading the notes and finding them on your instrument in no particular rhythm or tempo. A greater challenge can be achieved by playing them at a steady tempo or by playing them in a simple rhythmic pattern. Beginner students can begin by writing in the note names.
- Play each exercise in all 15 key signatures.
- Advanced theory students and improvising musicians can also use these exercises to practice identifying scale degrees in various keys or playing chords built on every scale degree in the chosen key.
- Develop comfort with chords by playing a chord built on each note in the exercise. For example: for each note in the exercise, play the major chord with that root. Increase the difficulty with different chord qualities or different chord tones, for example: for every note, play the minor 7th chord in which the given note is the 3rd.
- Practice transposing into different keys. This is an especially useful challenge for people who play transposing instruments such as brass and woodwind instruments.
- Chapters with wide ranges can present a great exercise for musicians who play instruments where large leaps are a challenge. People who play strings, mallet percussion, piano, woodwinds, and brass would be among those who would benefit from practising these awkward leaps and falls.

As with any of the Dots and Beams books, the uses for this particular collection are limited only by the imagination of the musician using it. I highly encourage anybody using this book to find as many uses for it as possible. My hope is that as you grow as a musician you will find ever more creative and challenging ways to use these materials so that you can return to these books for years and still find a valuable way to use them.

Chapter 1:

On the Staff
Diatonic

Exercise Range:

On the Staff - Diatonic
Exercise 1

On the Staff - Diatonic
Exercise 2

On the Staff - Diatonic
Exercise 3

On the Staff - Diatonic
Exercise 4

On the Staff - Diatonic
Exercise 6

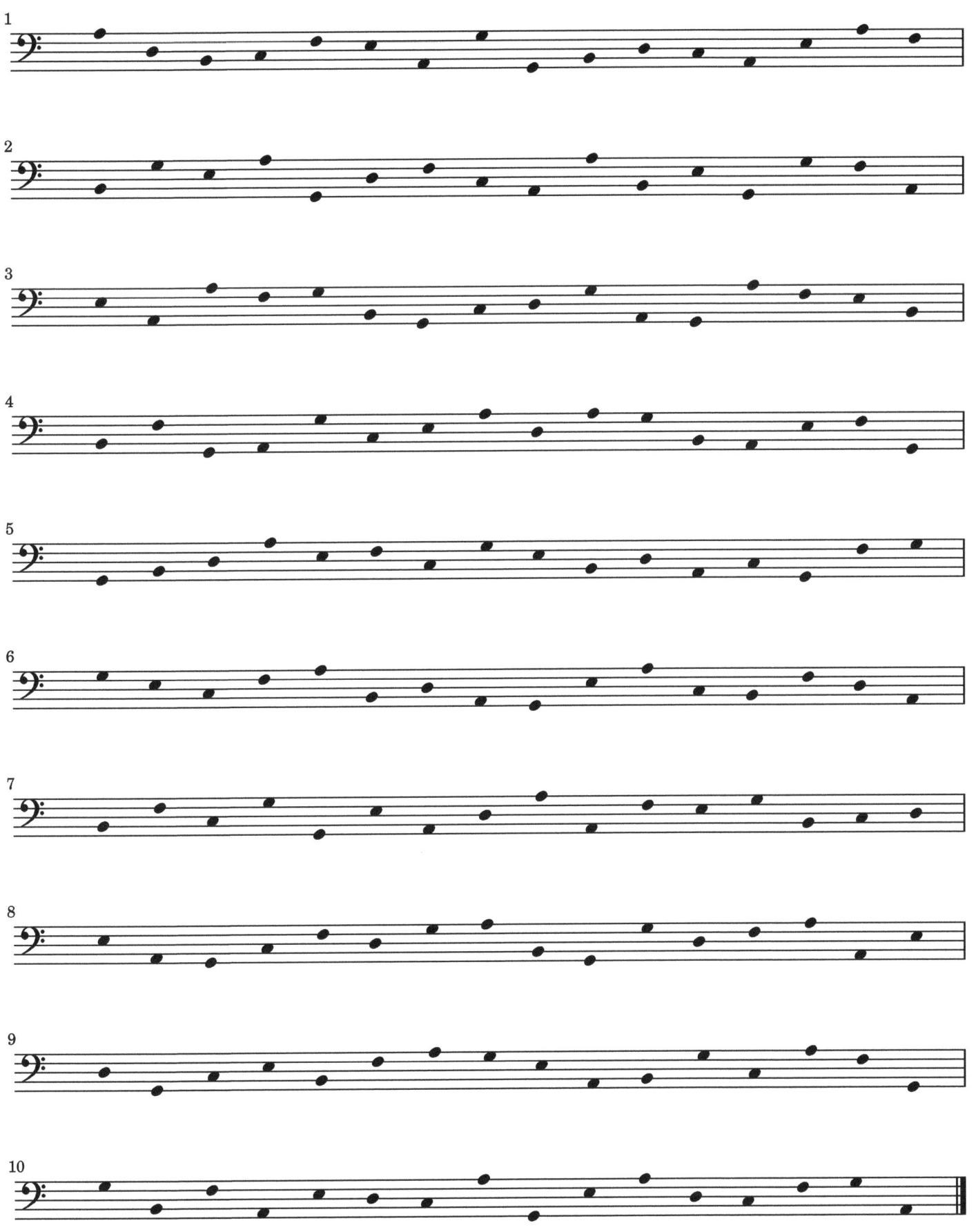

On the Staff - Diatonic
Exercise 7

Chapter 2:

On the Staff Chromatic

Exercise Range:

On the Staff - Chromatic
Exercise 1

On the Staff - Chromatic
Exercise 2

On the Staff - Chromatic
Exercise 3

On the Staff - Chromatic
Exercise 4

On the Staff - Chromatic
Exercise 5

On the Staff - Chromatic
Exercise 6 - Including B♯, C♭, E♯, F♭

On the Staff - Chromatic

Exercise 7 - Including B♯, C♭, E♯, F♭

On the Staff - Chromatic
Exercise 8 - Including B♯, C♭, E♯, F♭

On the Staff - Chromatic
Exercise 9 - Including B♯, C♭, E♯, F♭

Chapter 3:

Above the Staff
Diatonic

Exercise Ranges:

Above the Staff - Diatonic
Exercise 1 - First Ledger Line

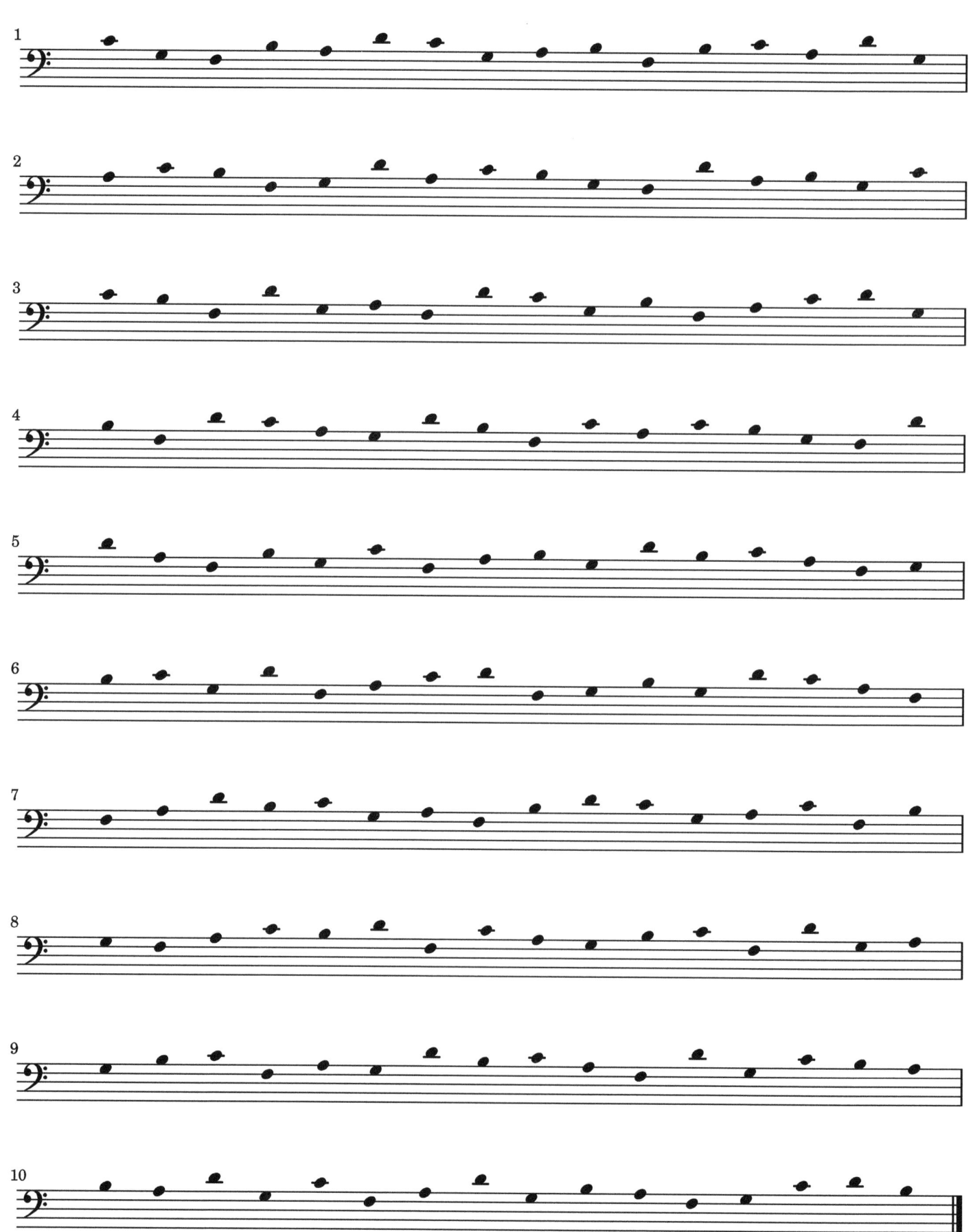

Above the Staff - Diatonic
Exercise 2 - First Ledger Line

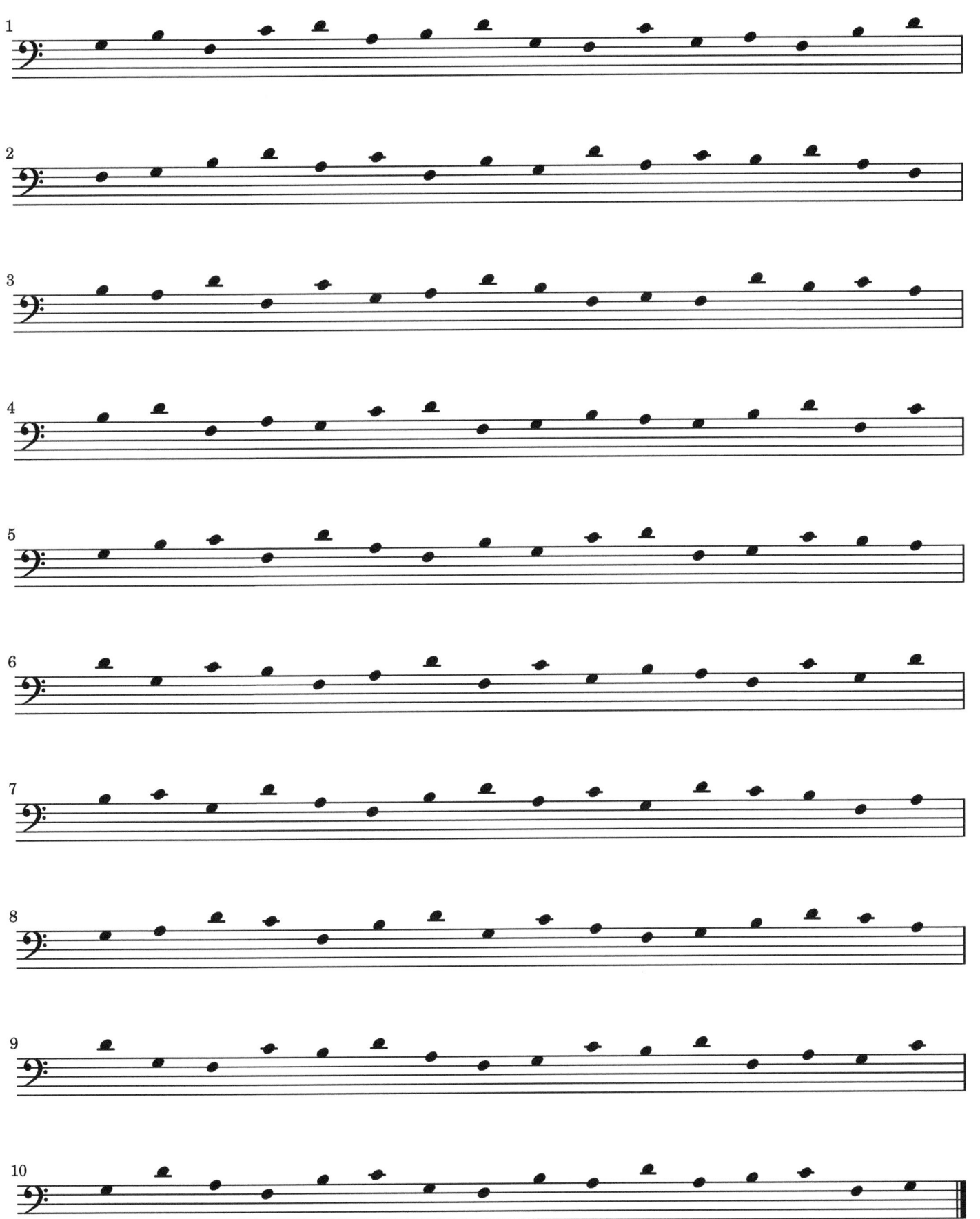

Above the Staff - Diatonic

Exercise 3 - First Ledger Line

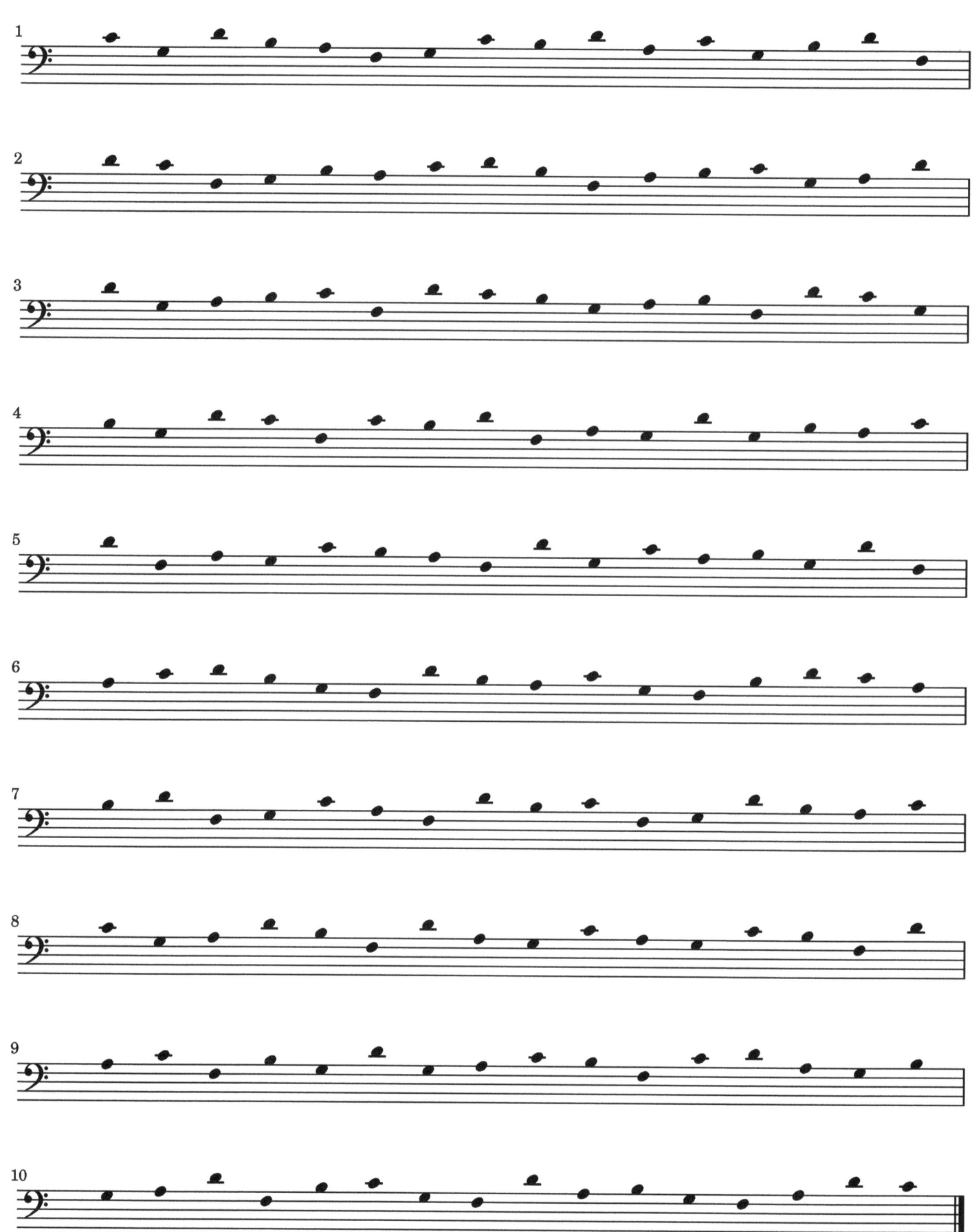

Above the Staff - Diatonic

Exercise 4 - Second Ledger Line

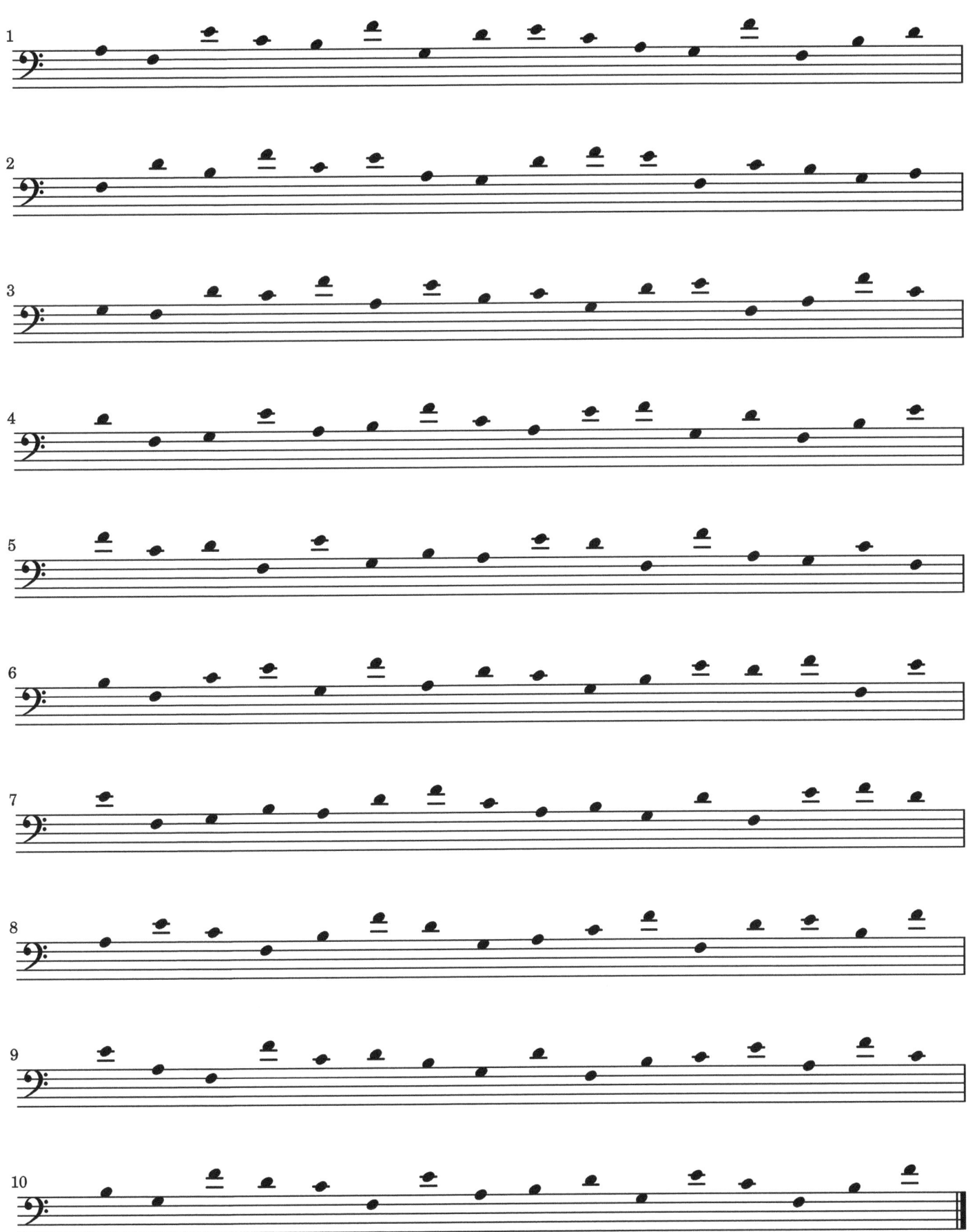

Above the Staff - Diatonic

Exercise 5 - Second Ledger Line

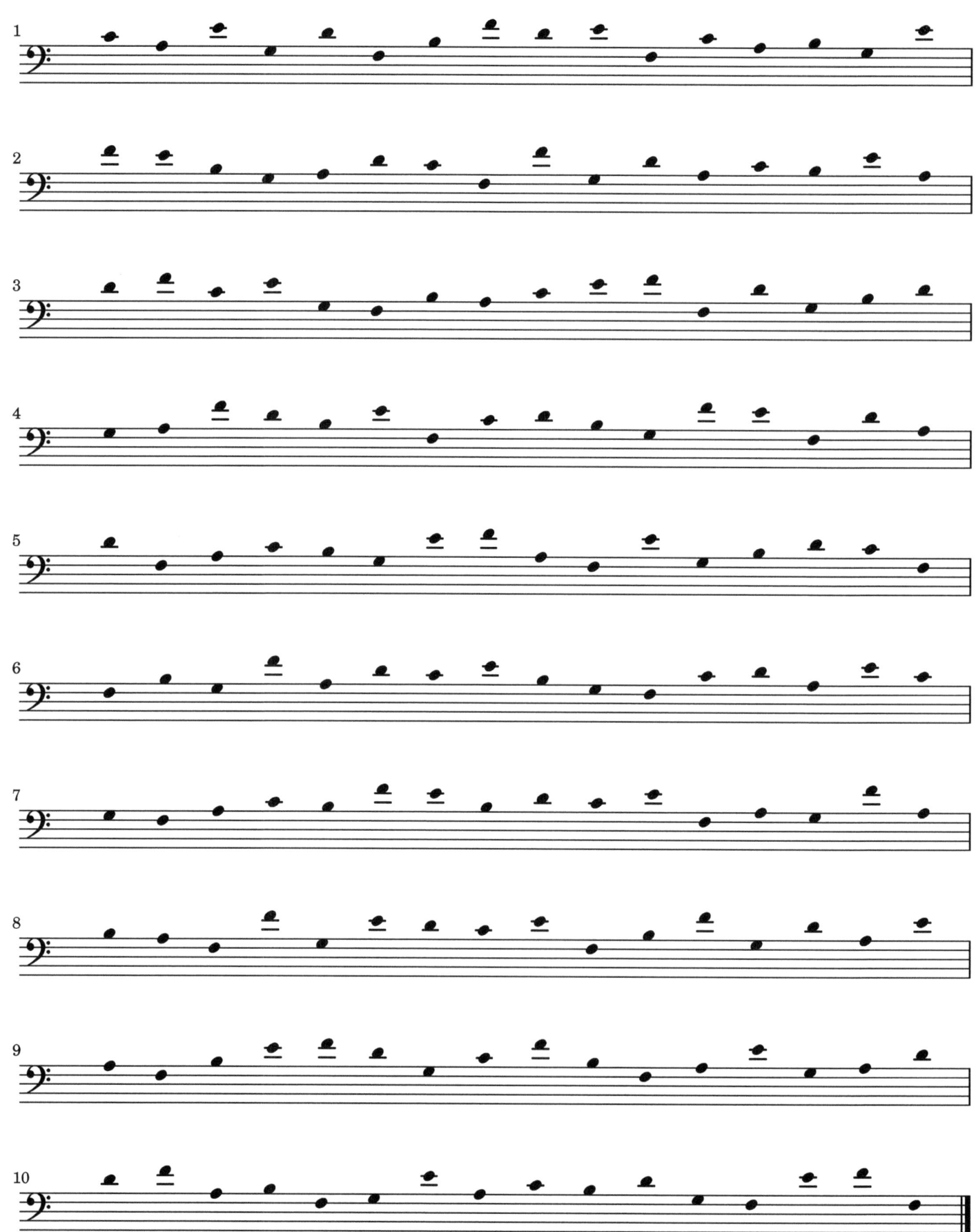

Above the Staff - Diatonic

Exercise 6 - Second Ledger Line

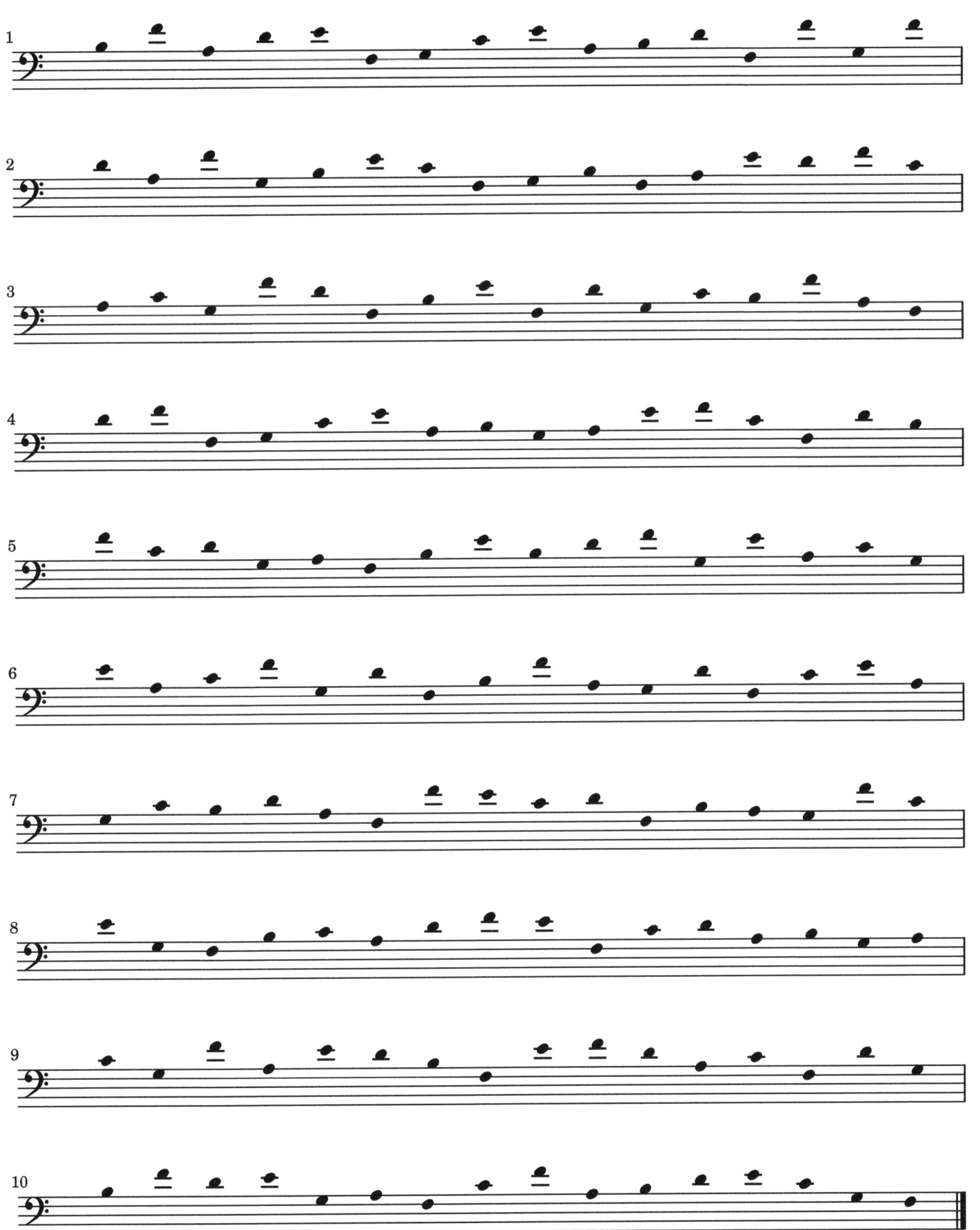

Above the Staff - Diatonic

Exercise 7 - Third Ledger Line

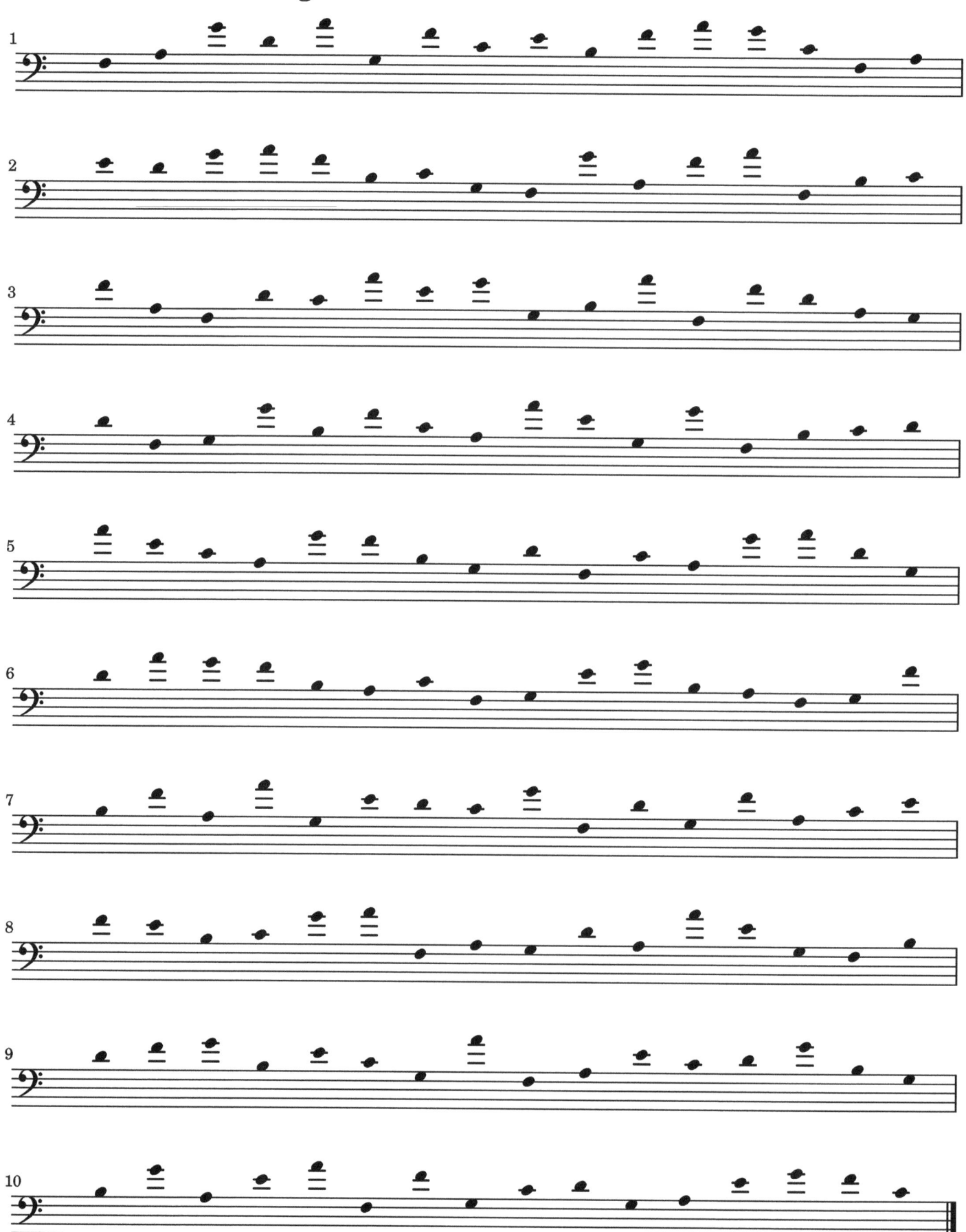

Above the Staff - Diatonic

Exercise 8 - Third Ledger Line

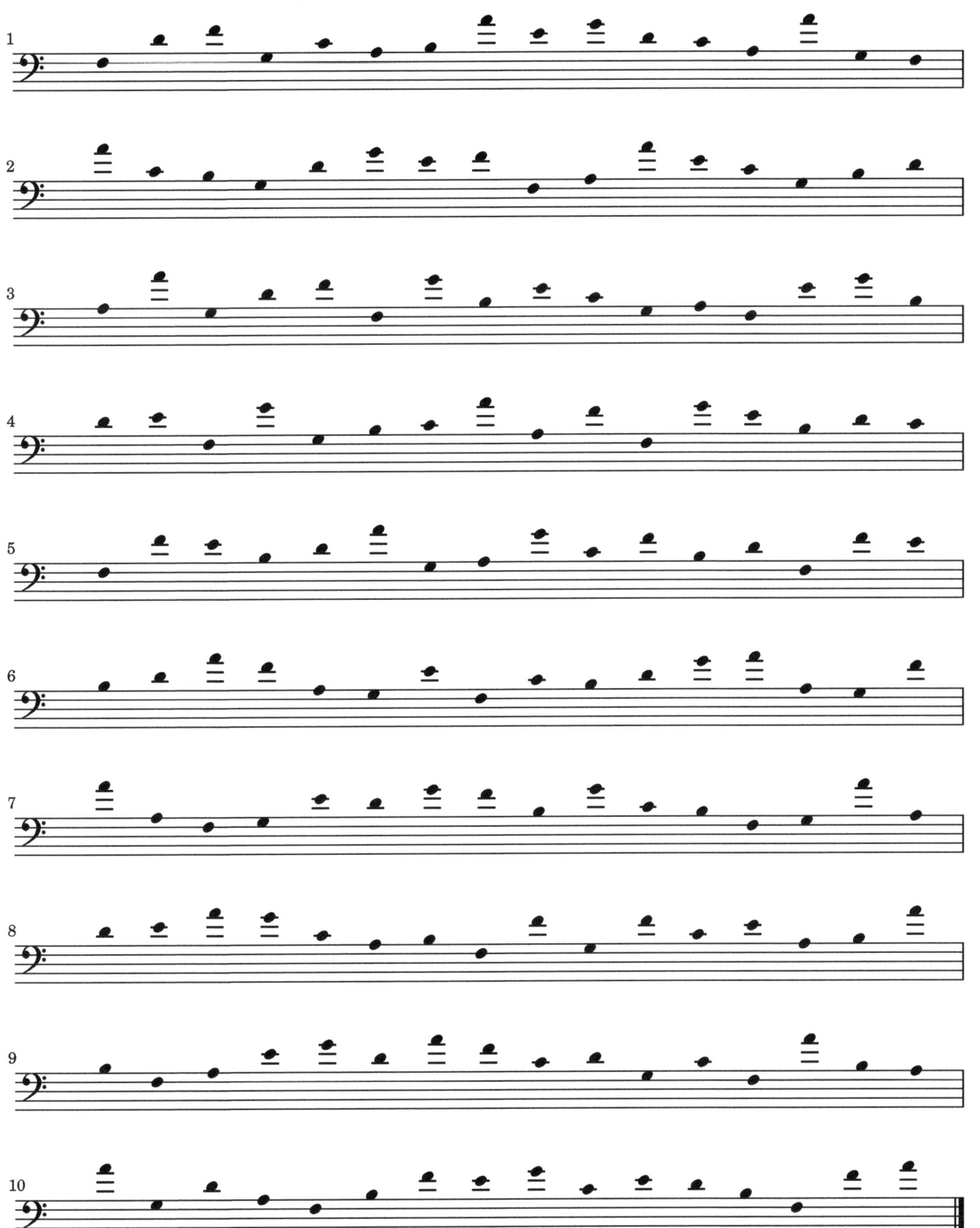

Above the Staff - Diatonic

Exercise 9 - Third Ledger Line

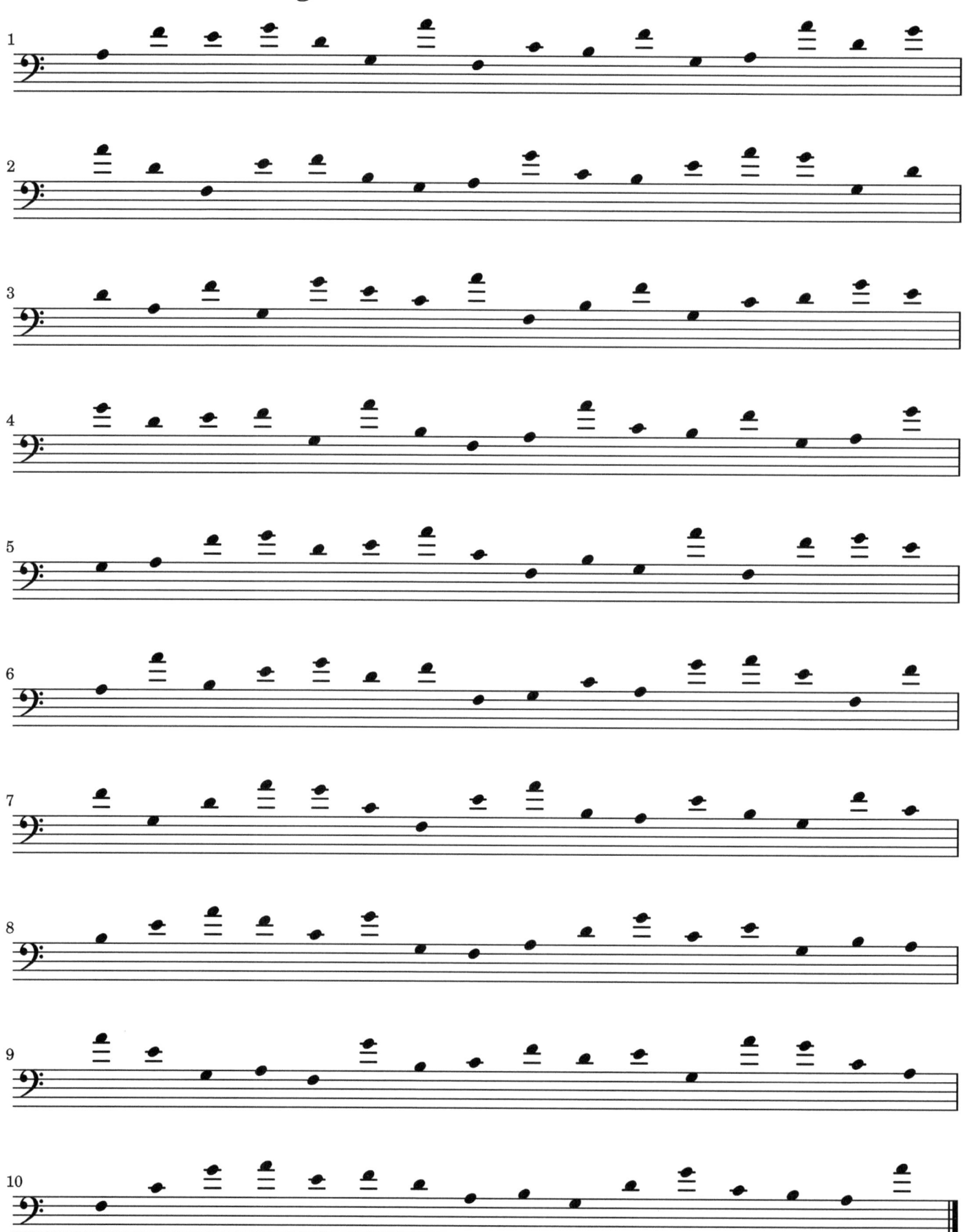

Above the Staff - Diatonic

Exercise 10 - Fourth Ledger Line

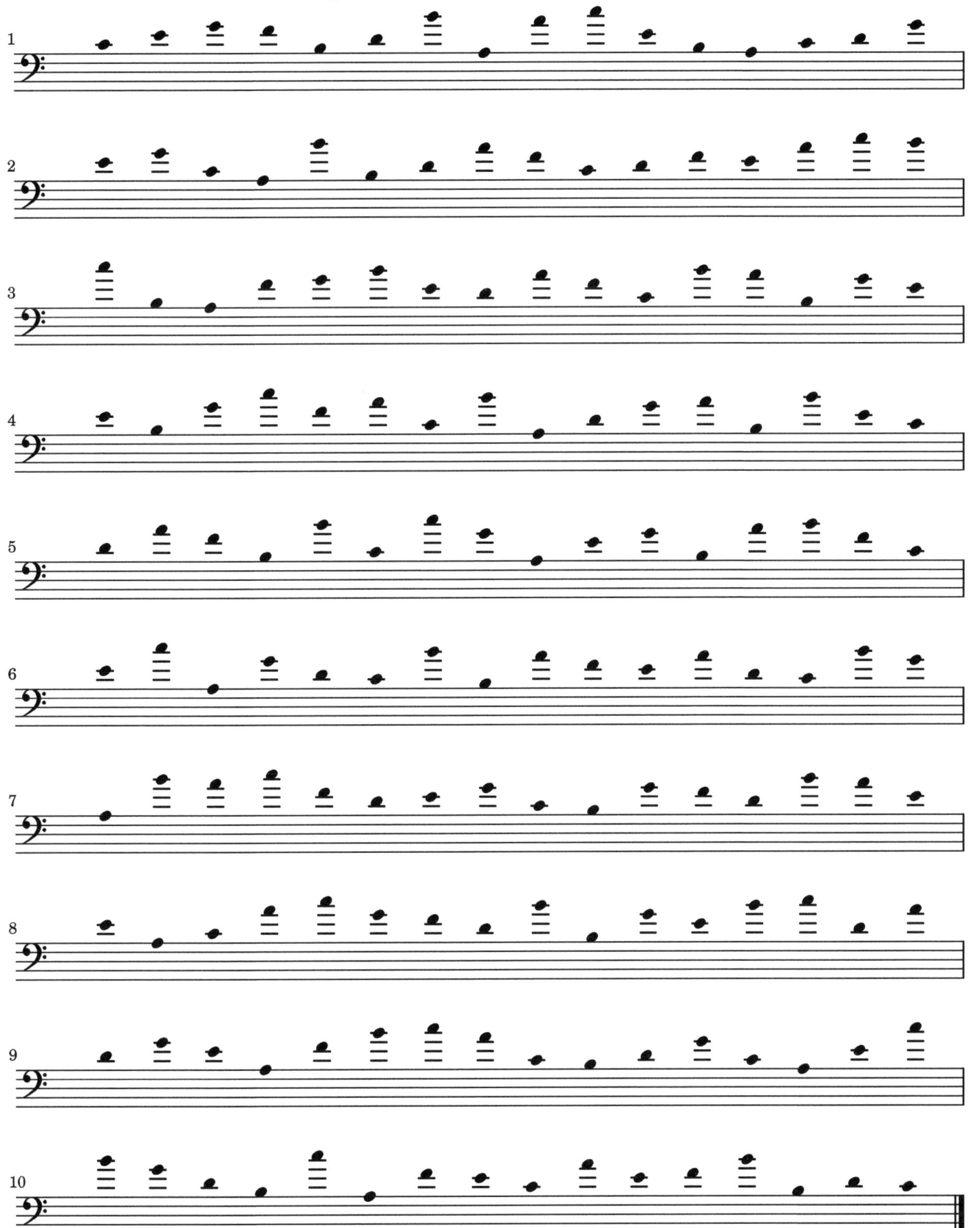

Above the Staff - Diatonic

Exercise 11 - Fourth Ledger Line

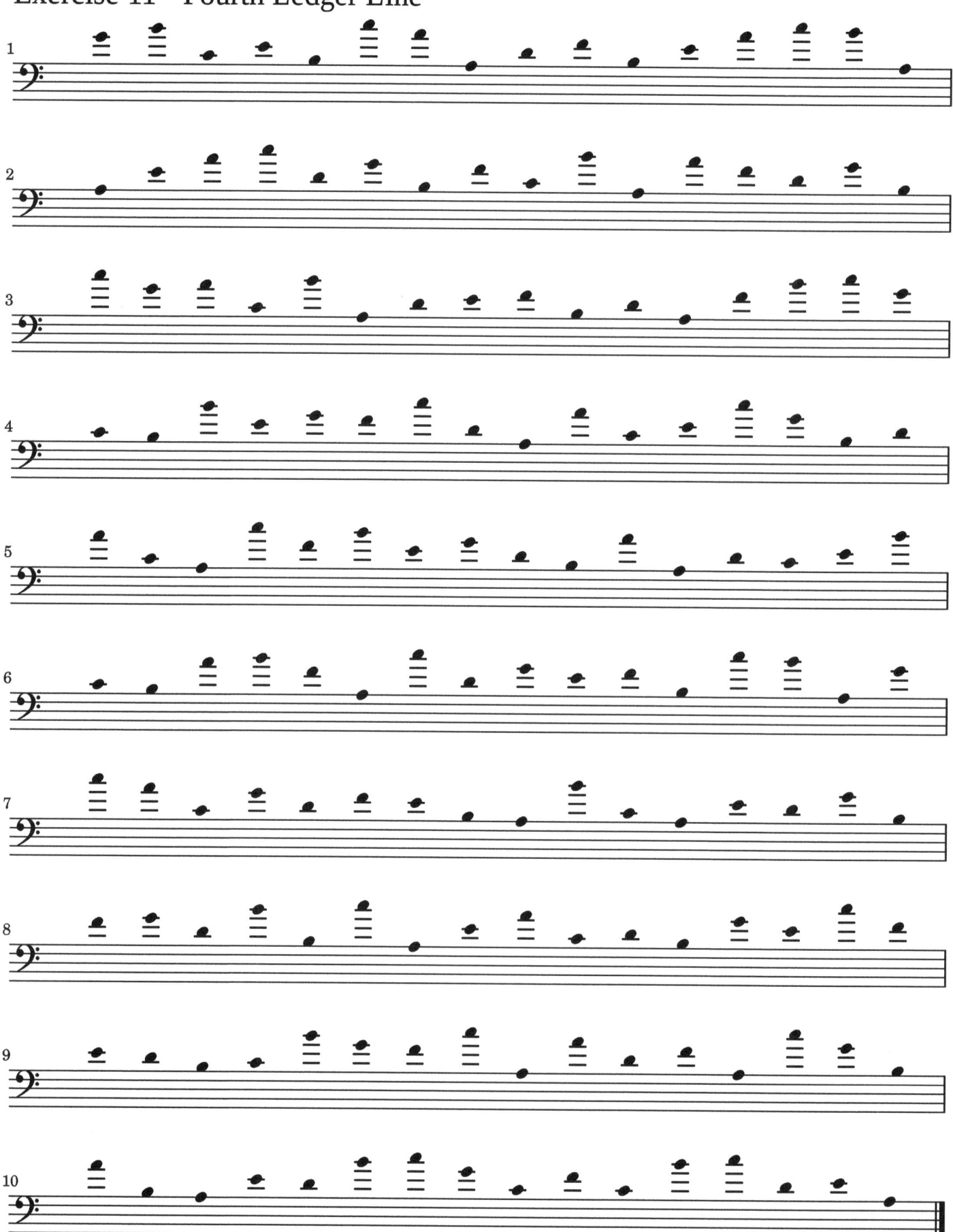

Above the Staff - Diatonic
Exercise 12 - Fourth Ledger Line

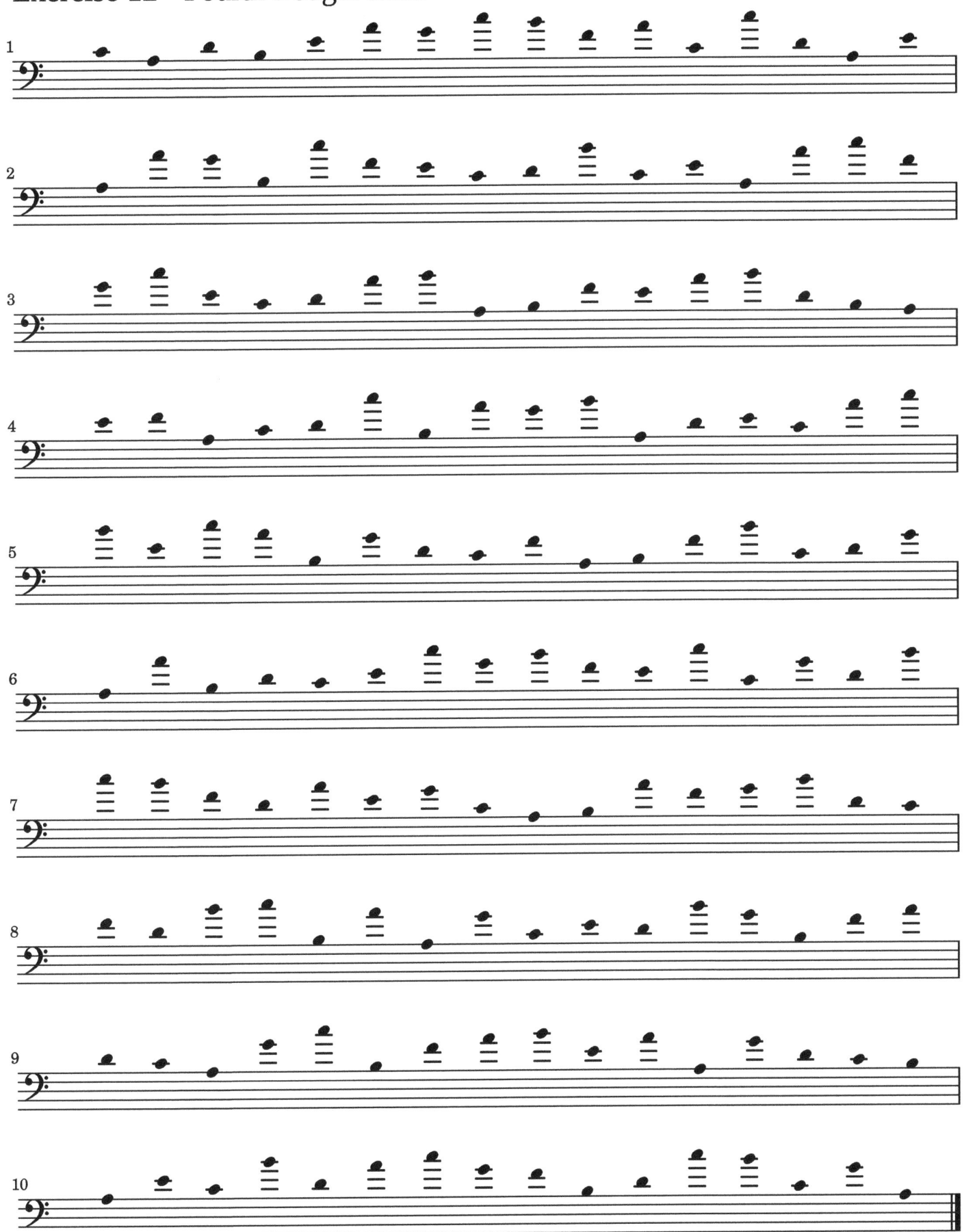

Chapter 4:

Above the Staff Chromatic

Exercise Ranges:

Above the Staff - Chromatic

Exercise 1 - First Ledger Line

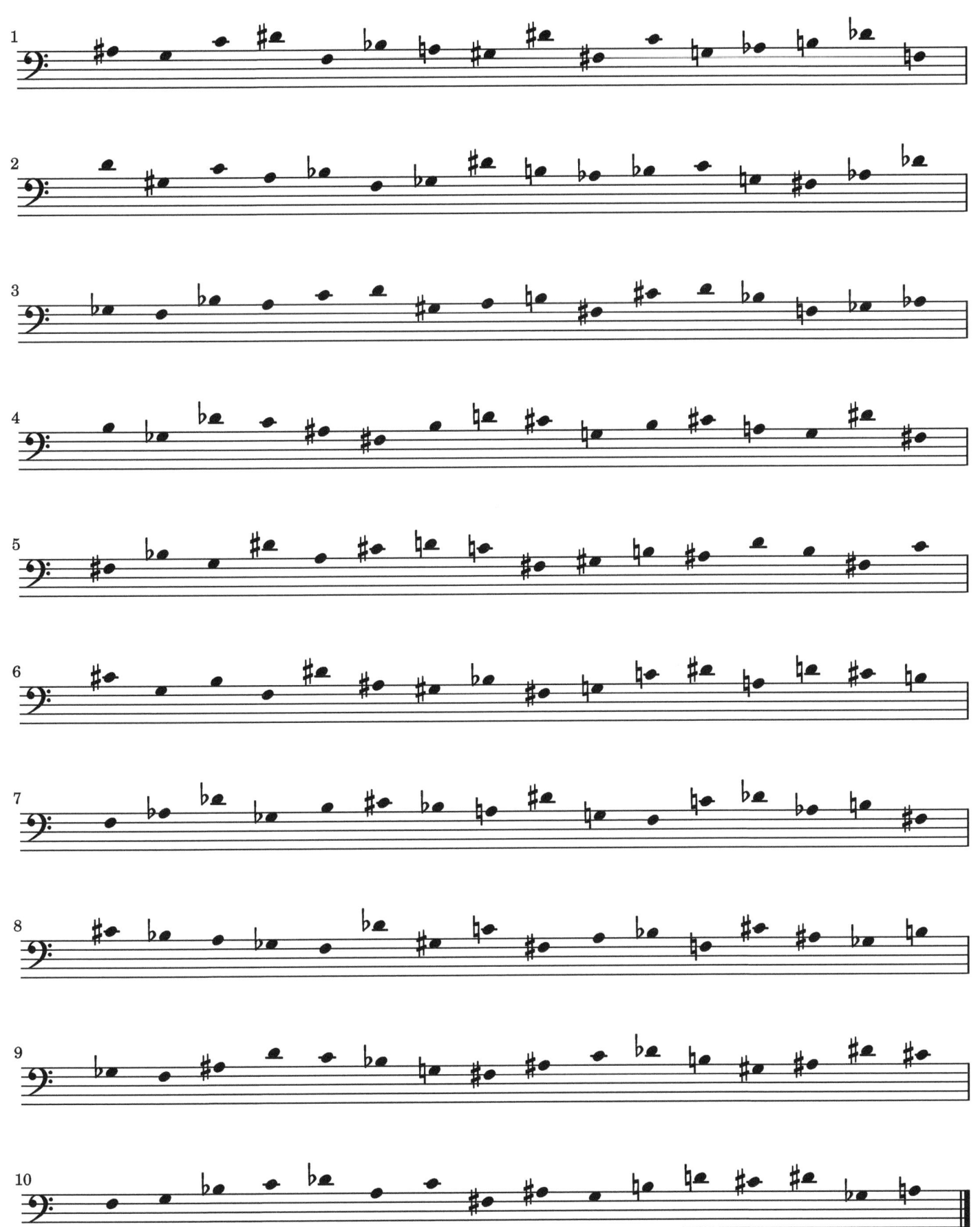

Above the Staff - Chromatic

Exercise 2 - First Ledger Line

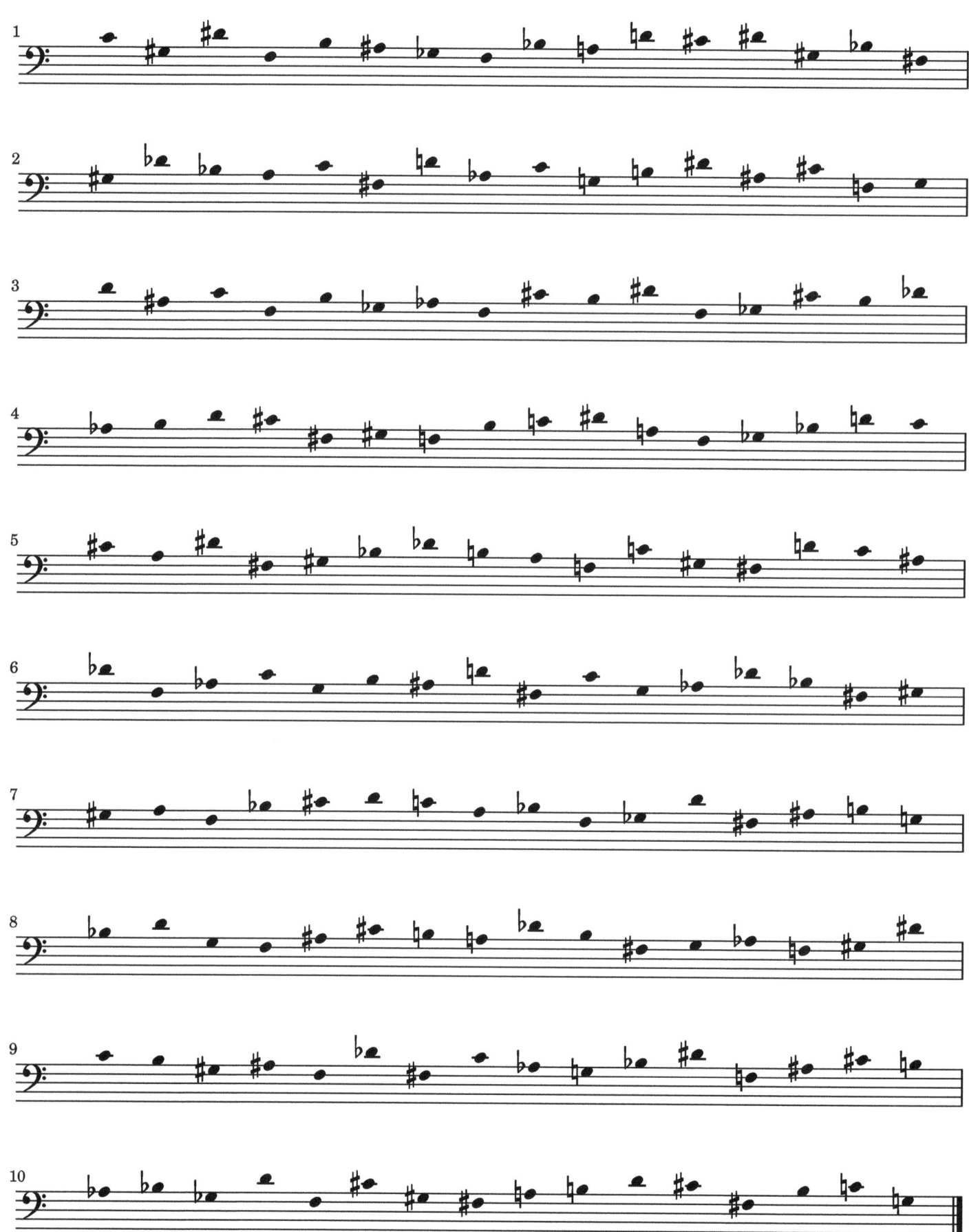

Above the Staff - Chromatic

Exercise 3 - First Ledger Line - Including B#, C♭, E#, F♭

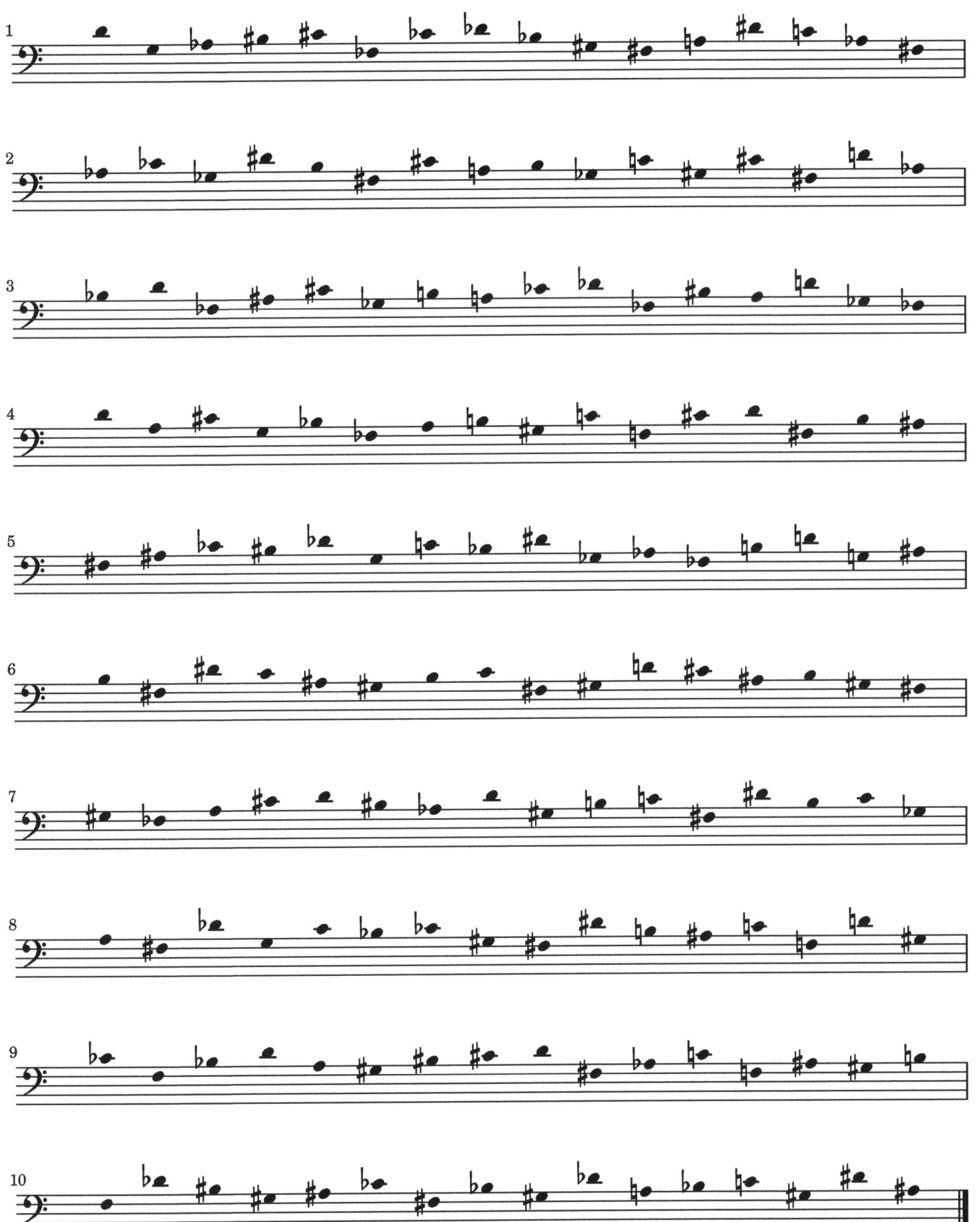

Above the Staff - Chromatic
Exercise 4 - Second Ledger Line

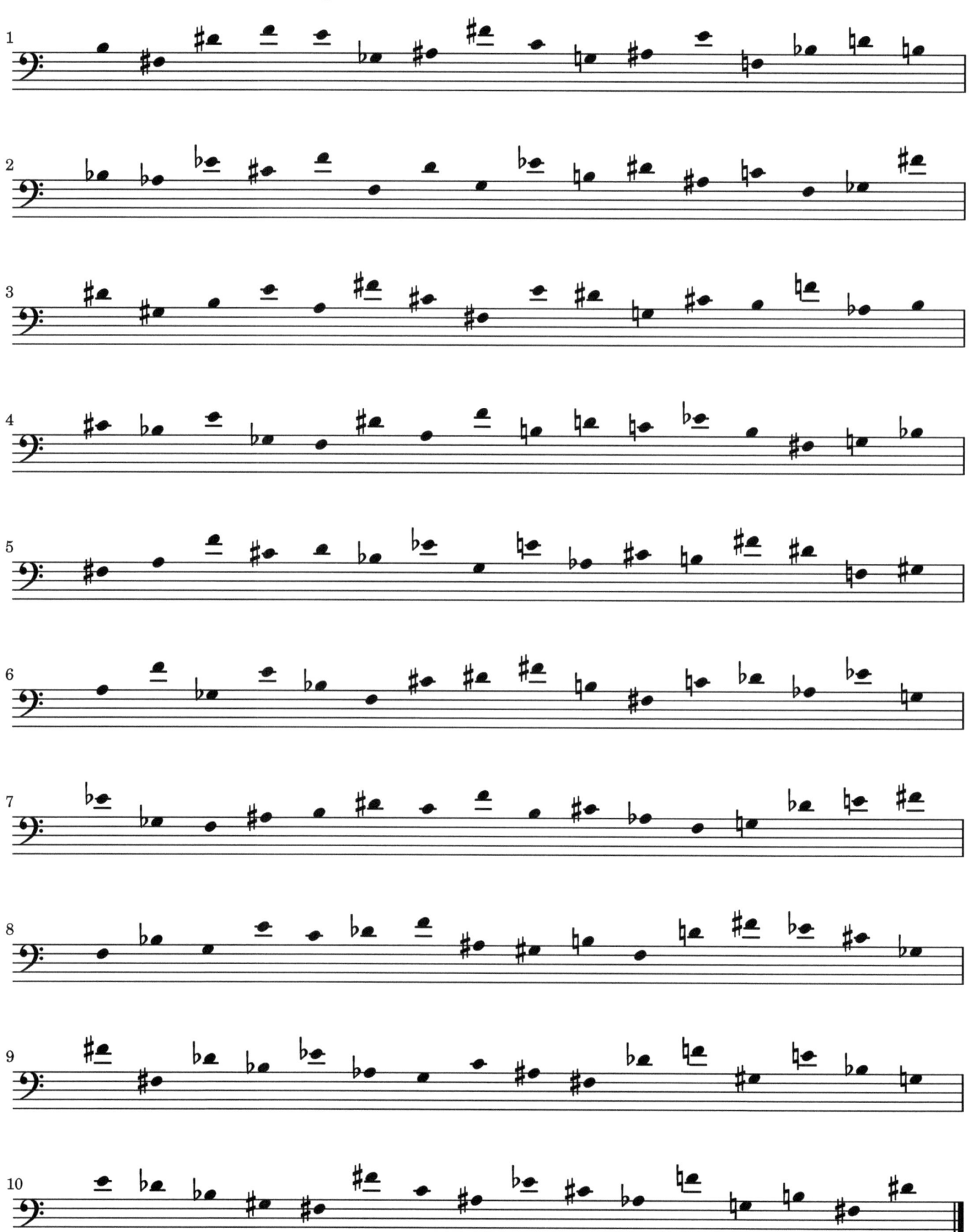

Above the Staff - Chromatic

Exercise 5 - Second Ledger Line

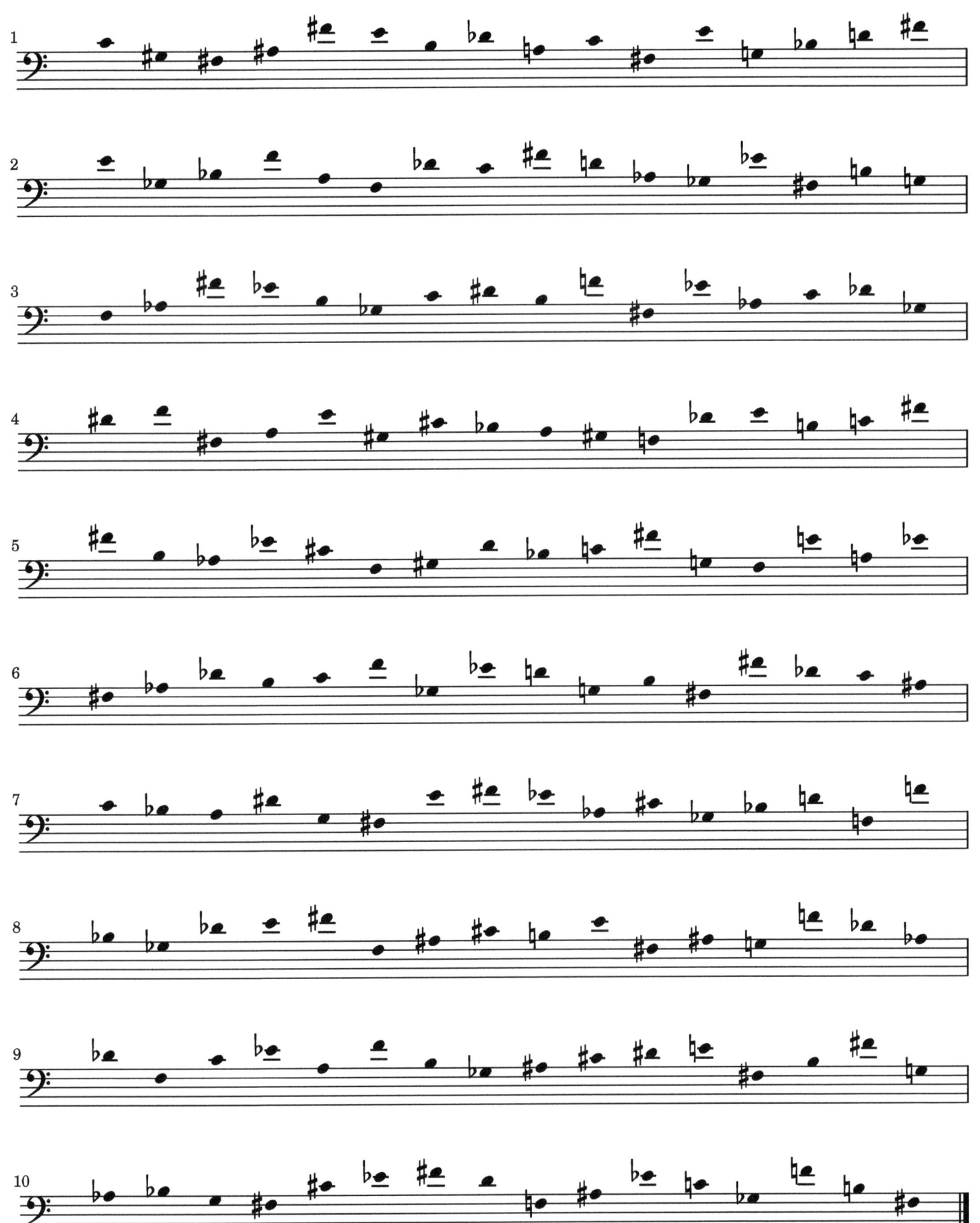

Above the Staff - Chromatic

Exercise 6 - Second Ledger Line - Including B#, C♭, E#, F♭

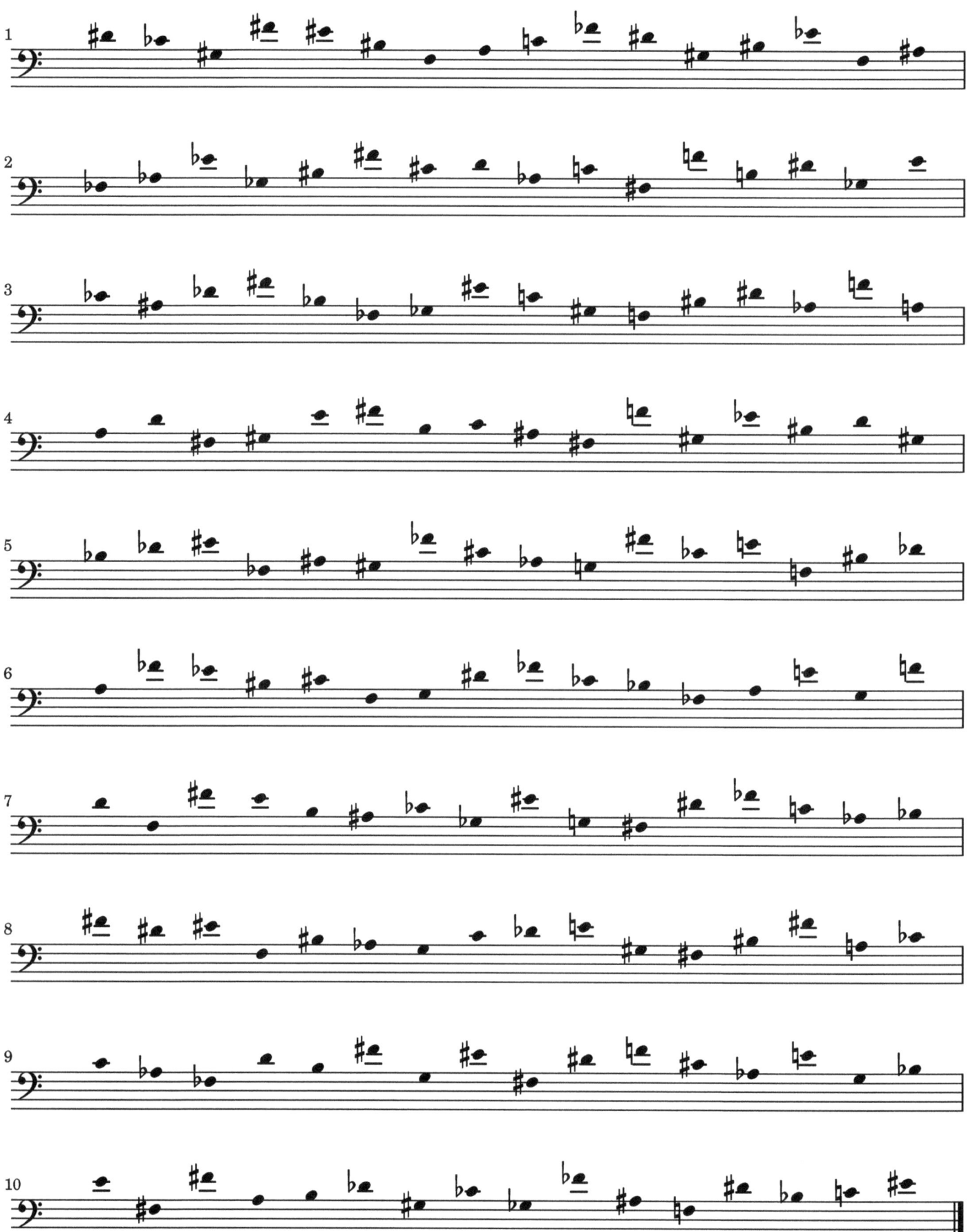

Above the Staff - Chromatic

Exercise 7 - Third Ledger Line

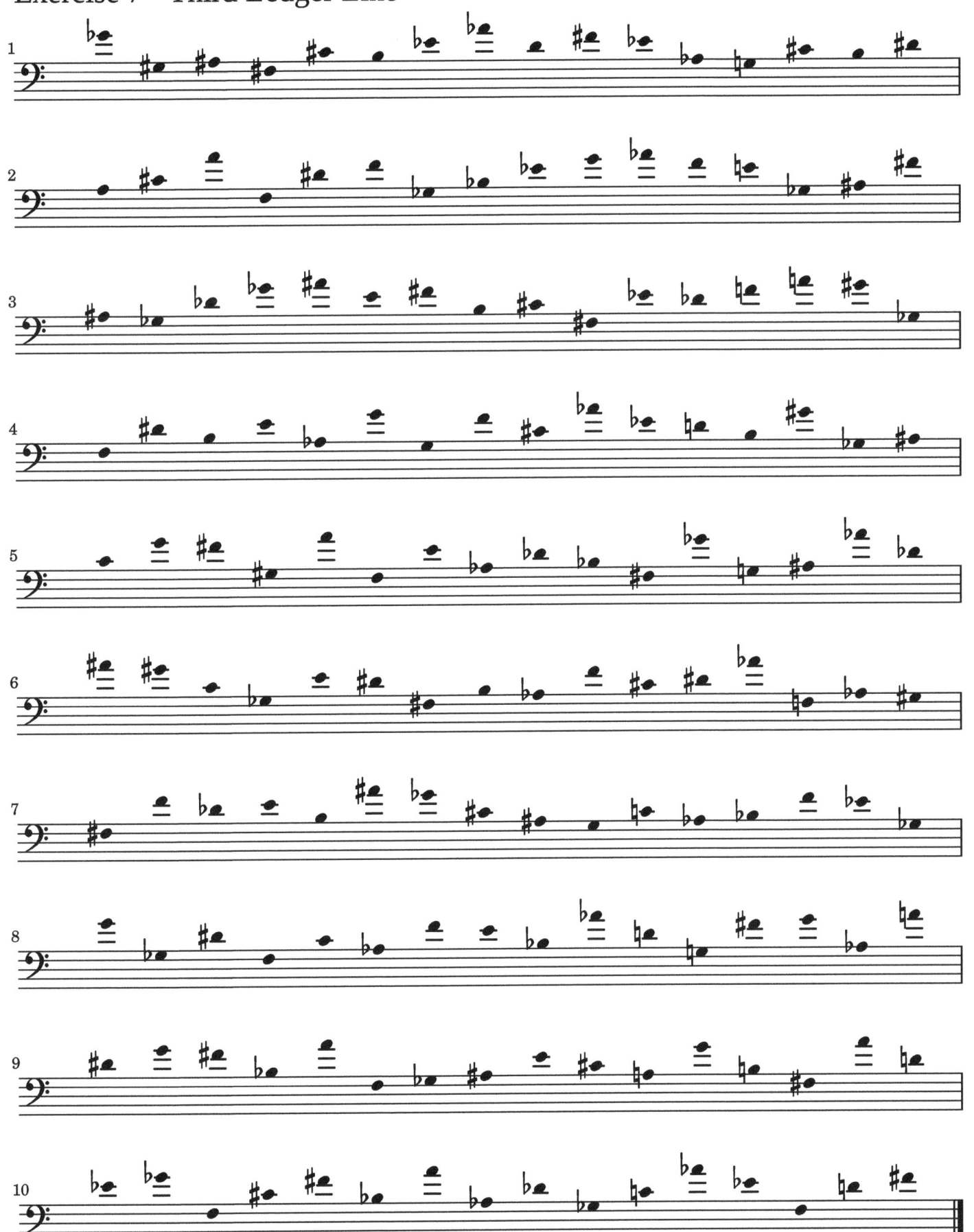

Above the Staff - Chromatic
Exercise 8 - Third Ledger Line

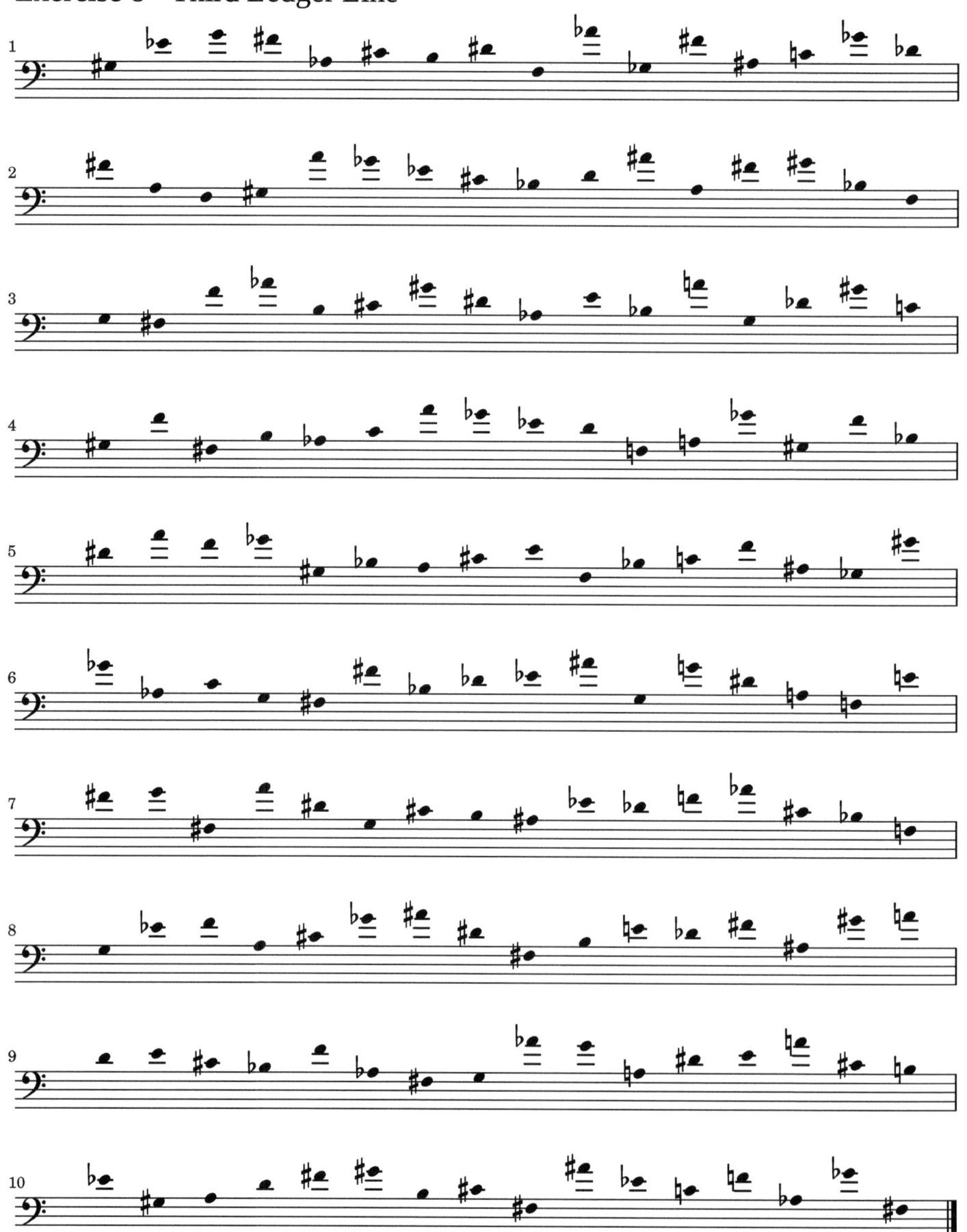

Above the Staff - Chromatic

Exercise 9 - Third Ledger Line - Including B#, C♭, E#, F♭

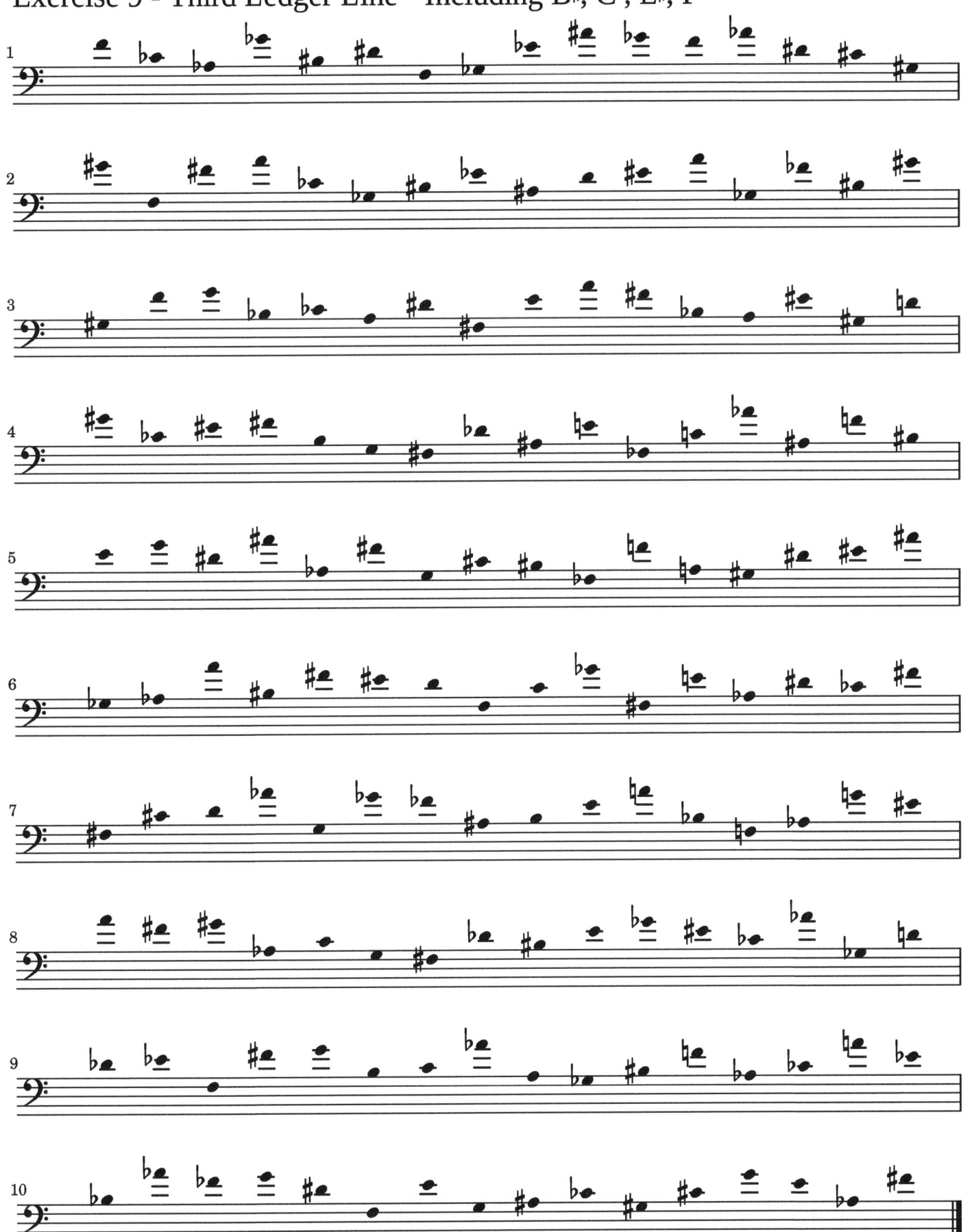

Above the Staff - Chromatic

Exercise 10 - Fourth Ledger Line

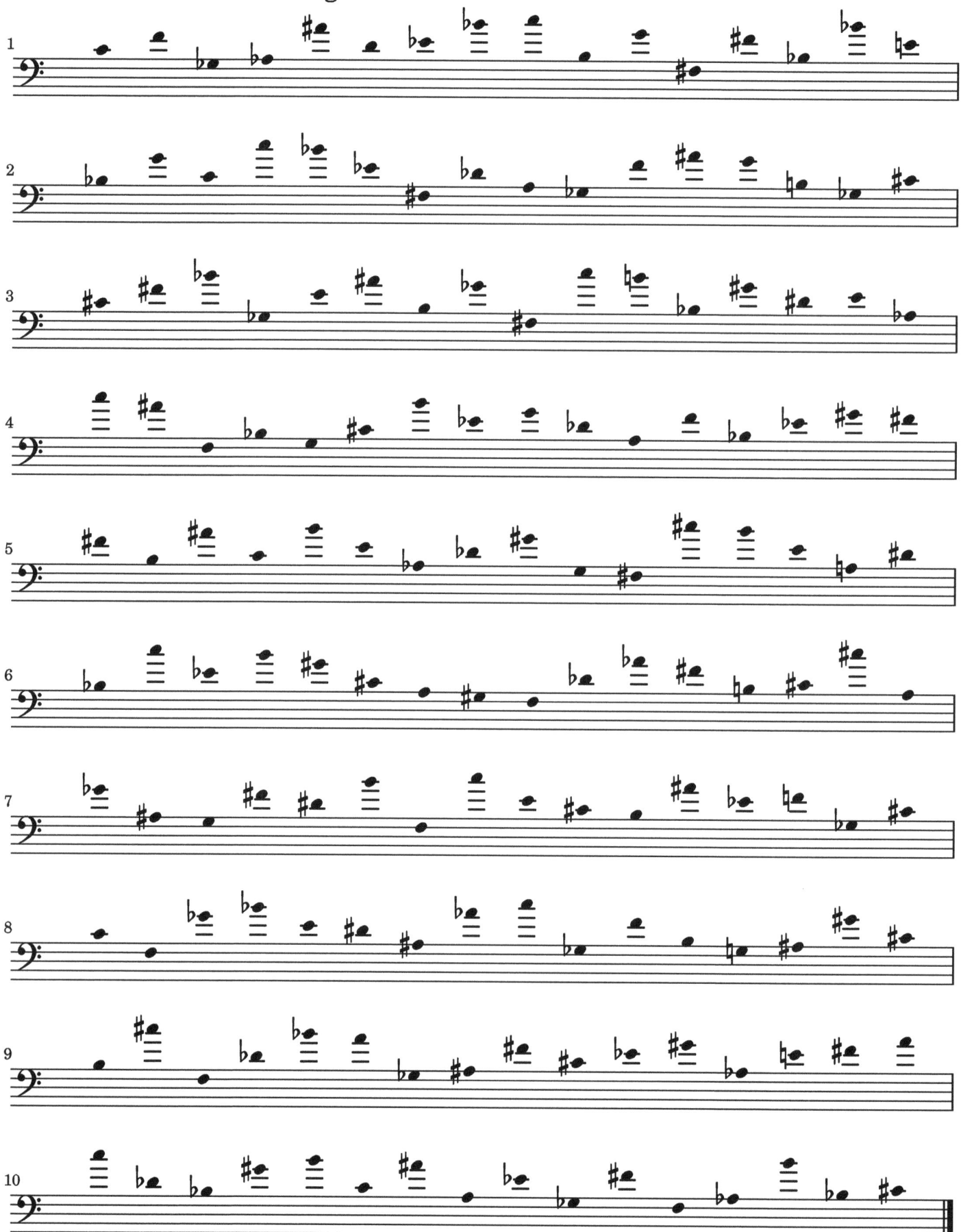

Above the Staff - Chromatic

Exercise 11 - Fourth Ledger Line

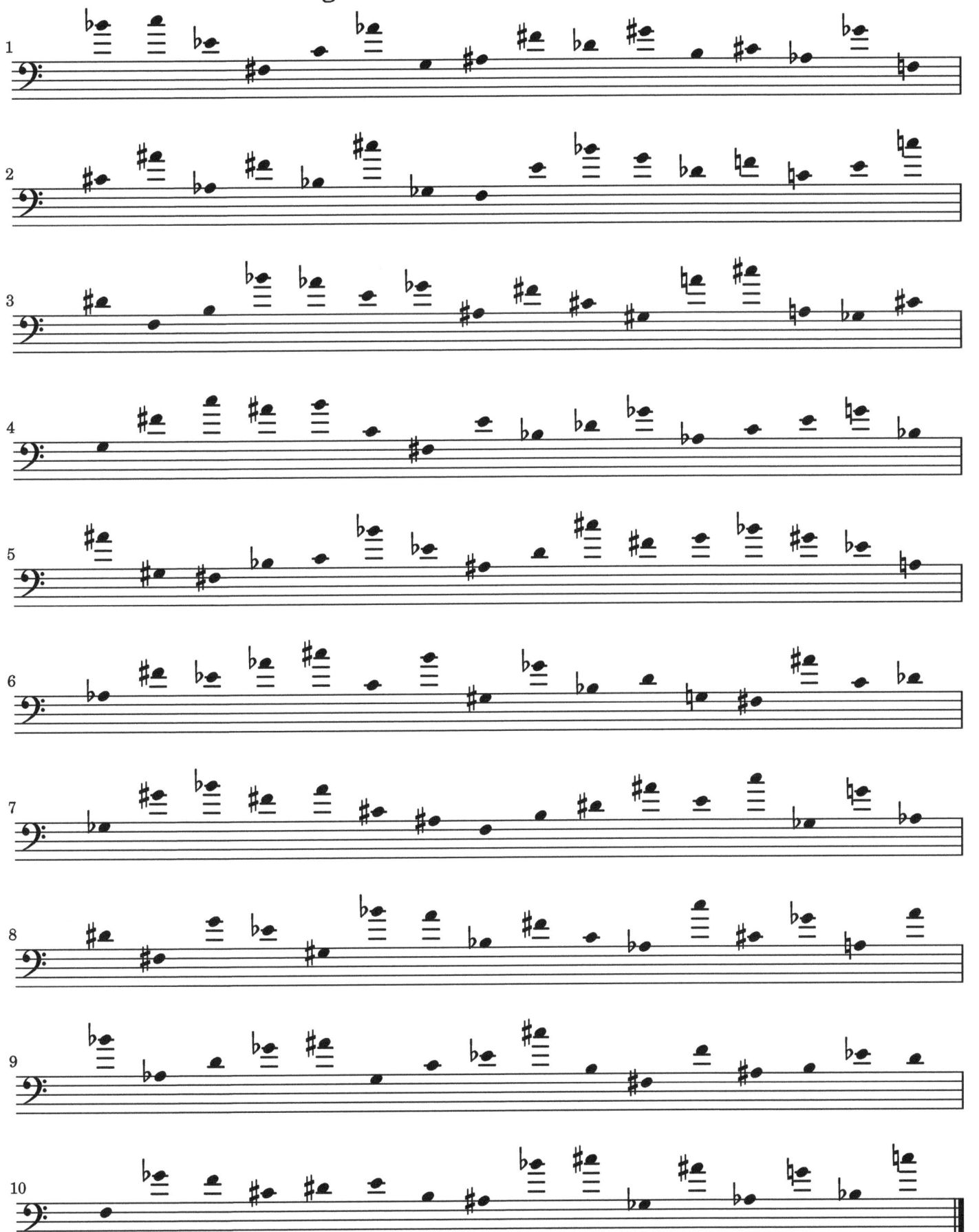

45

Above the Staff - Chromatic

Exercise 12 - Fourth Ledger Line - Including B#, C♭, E#, F♭

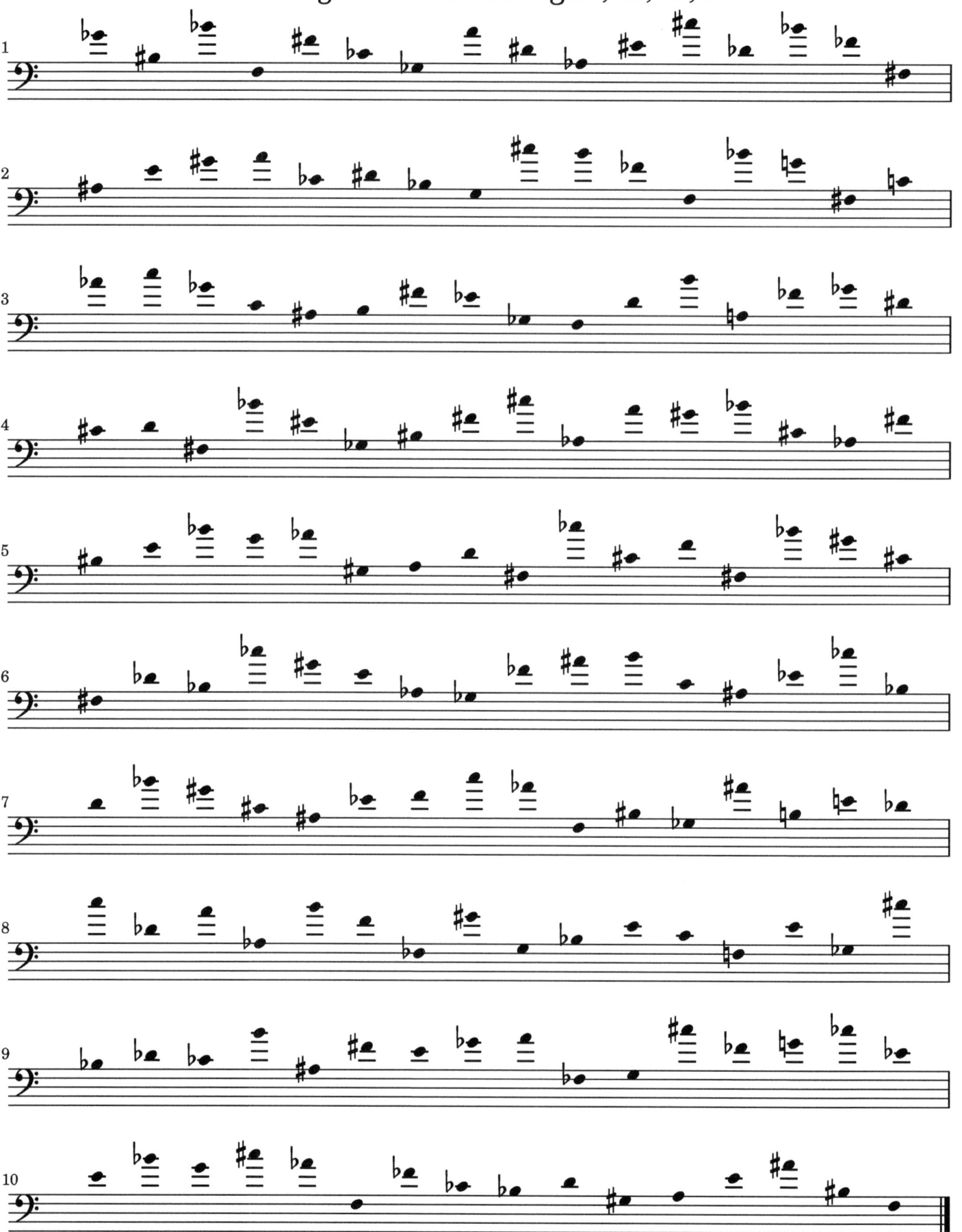

Chapter 5:

Below the Staff Diatonic

Exercise Ranges:

Below the Staff - Diatonic

Exercise 1 - First Ledger Line

48

Below the Staff - Diatonic
Exercise 2 - First Ledger Line

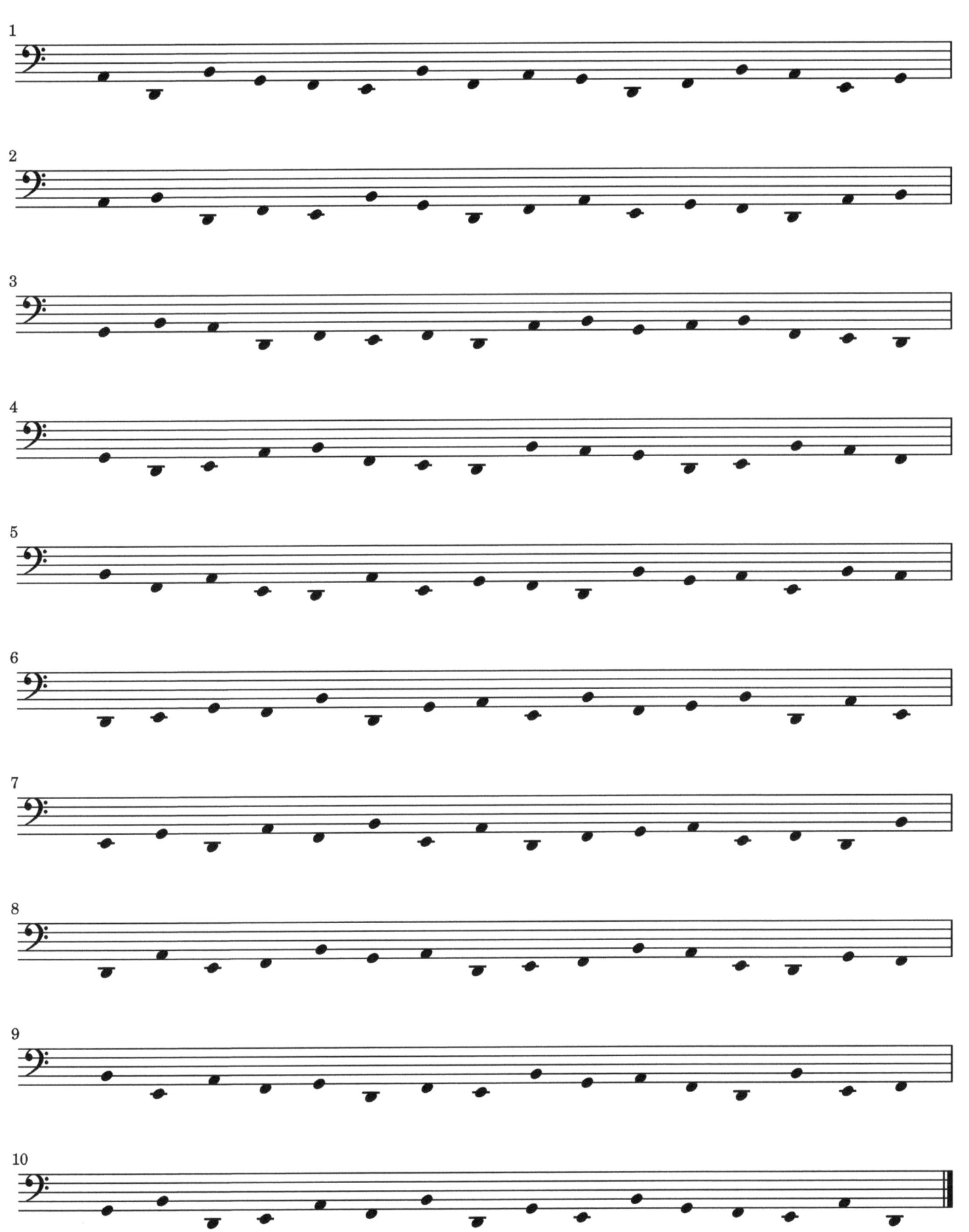

Below the Staff - Diatonic
Exercise 4 - Second Ledger Line

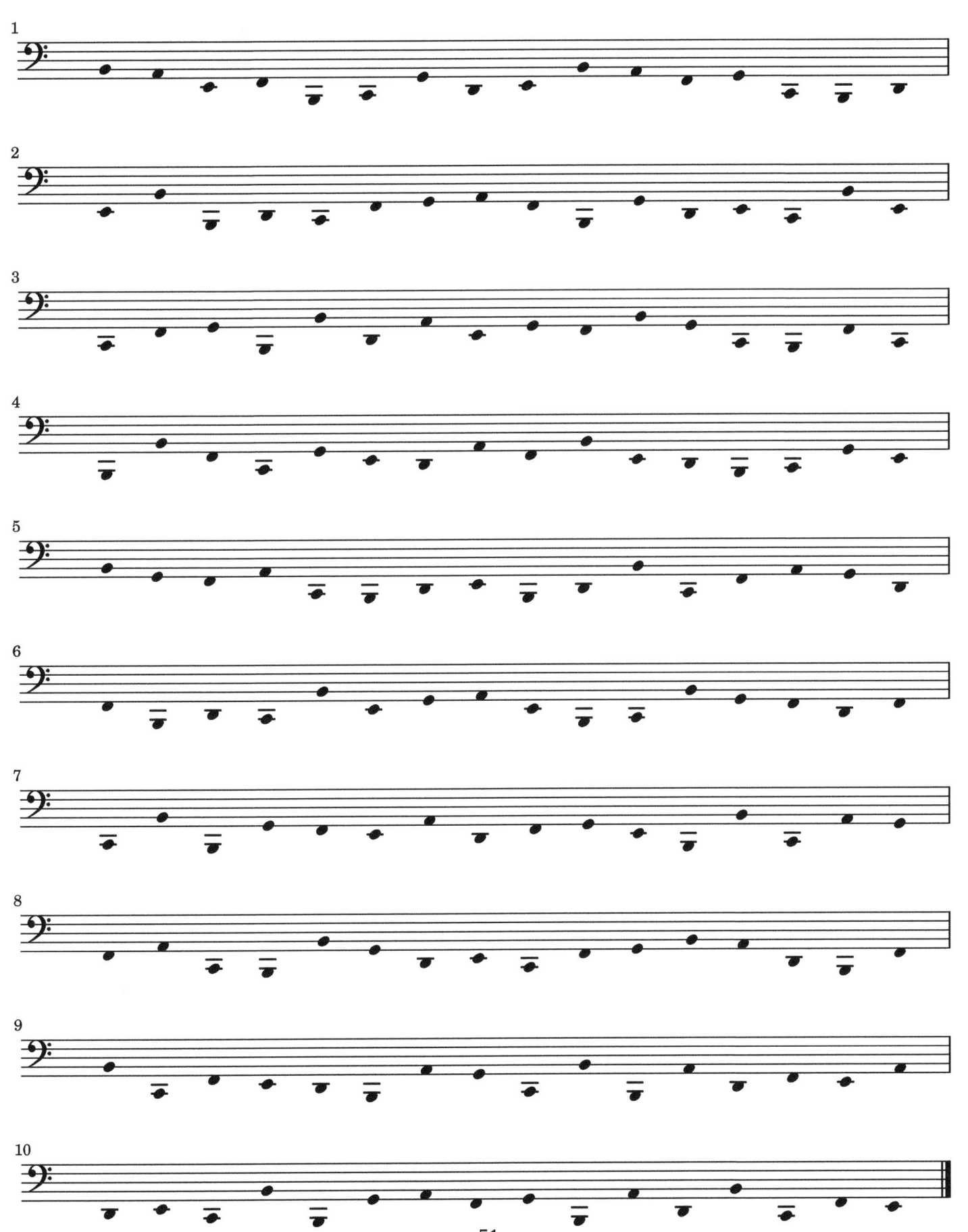

Below the Staff - Diatonic

Exercise 5 - Second Ledger Line

Below the Staff - Diatonic
Exercise 6 - Second Ledger Line

www.DotsandBeams.com

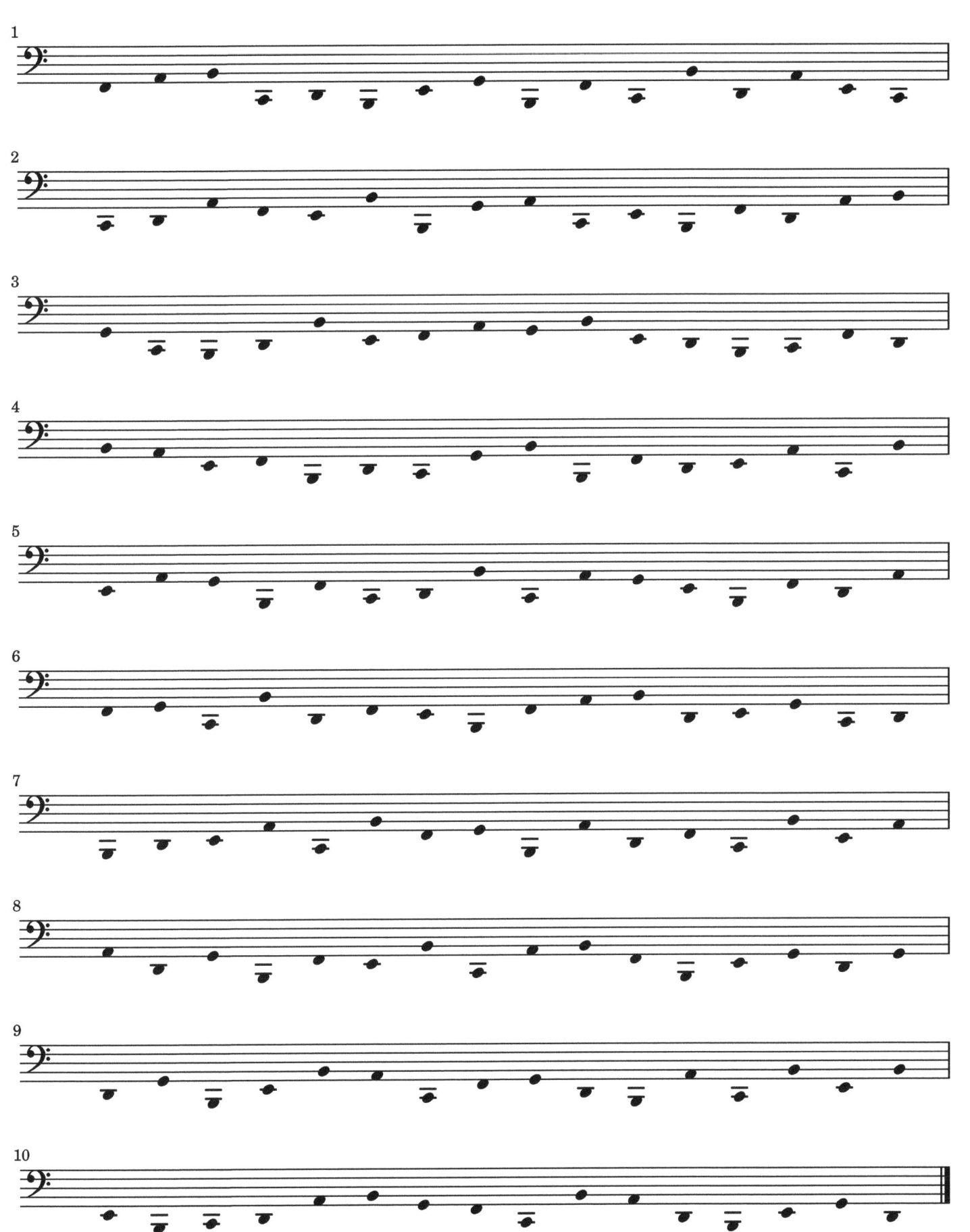

Below the Staff - Diatonic

Exercise 7 - Third Ledger Line

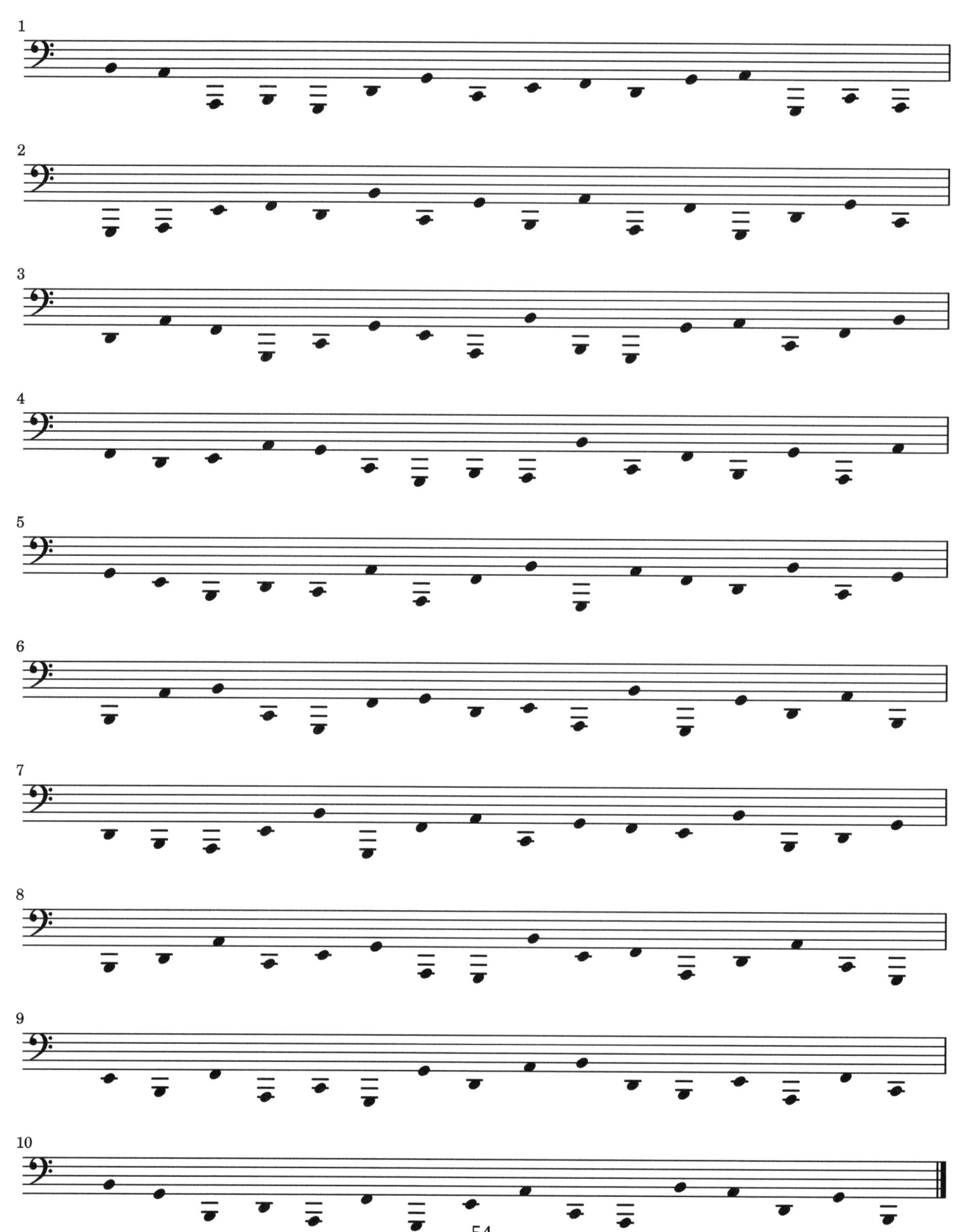

Below the Staff - Diatonic
Exercise 8 - Third Ledger Line

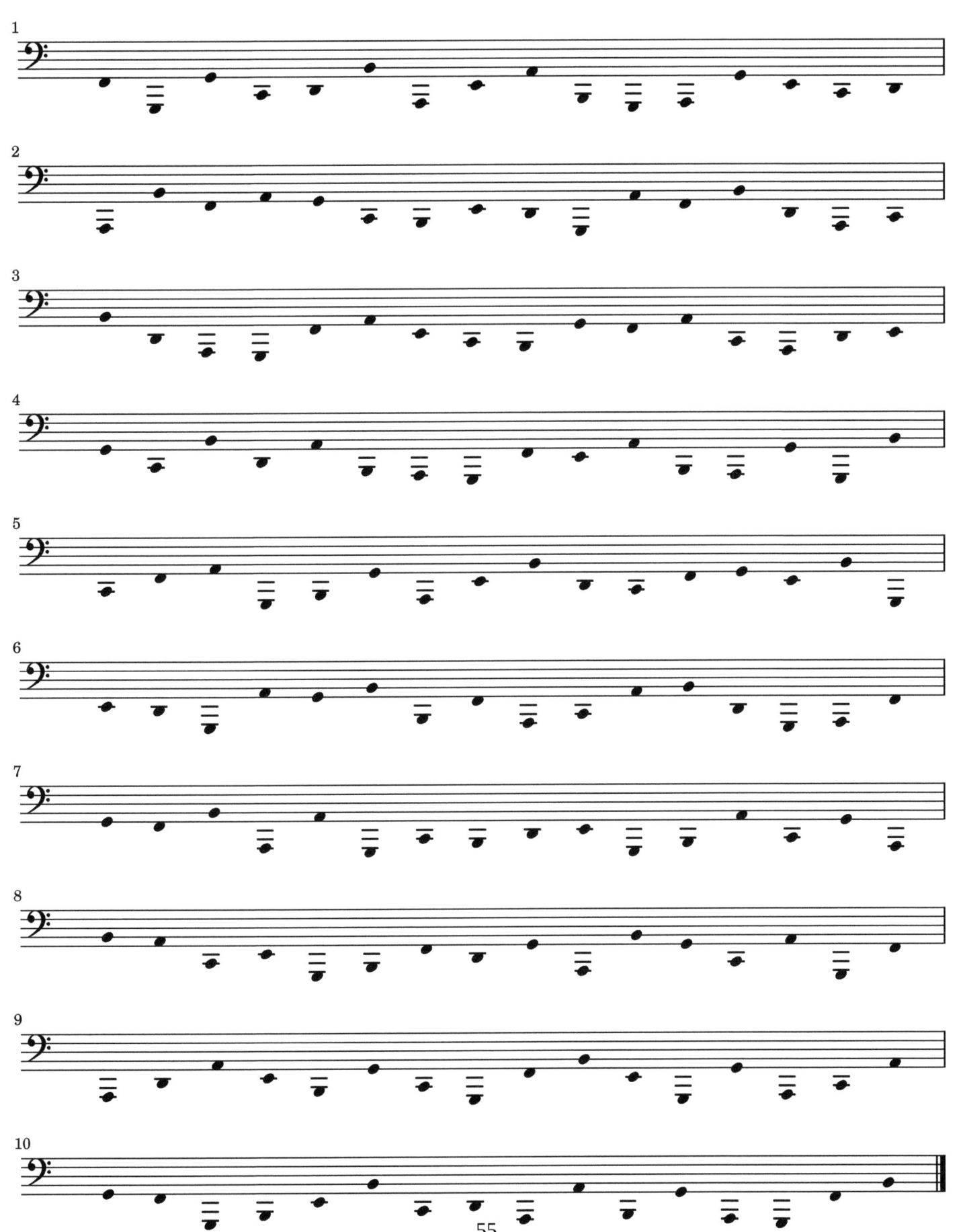

Below the Staff - Diatonic
Exercise 9 - Third Ledger Line

www.DotsandBeams.com

Below the Staff - Diatonic

Exercise 10 - Fourth Ledger Line

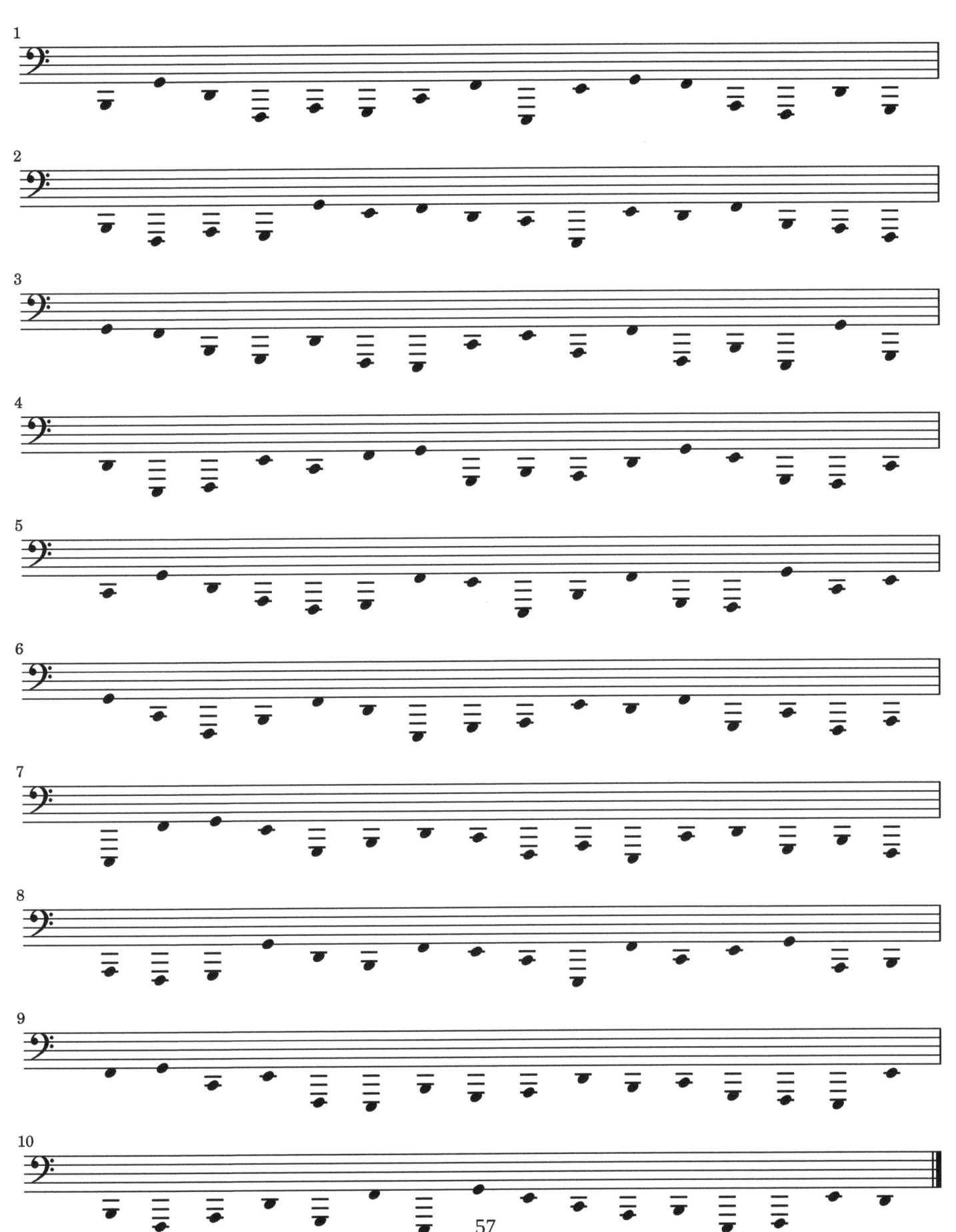

Below the Staff - Diatonic
Exercise 11 - Fourth Ledger Line

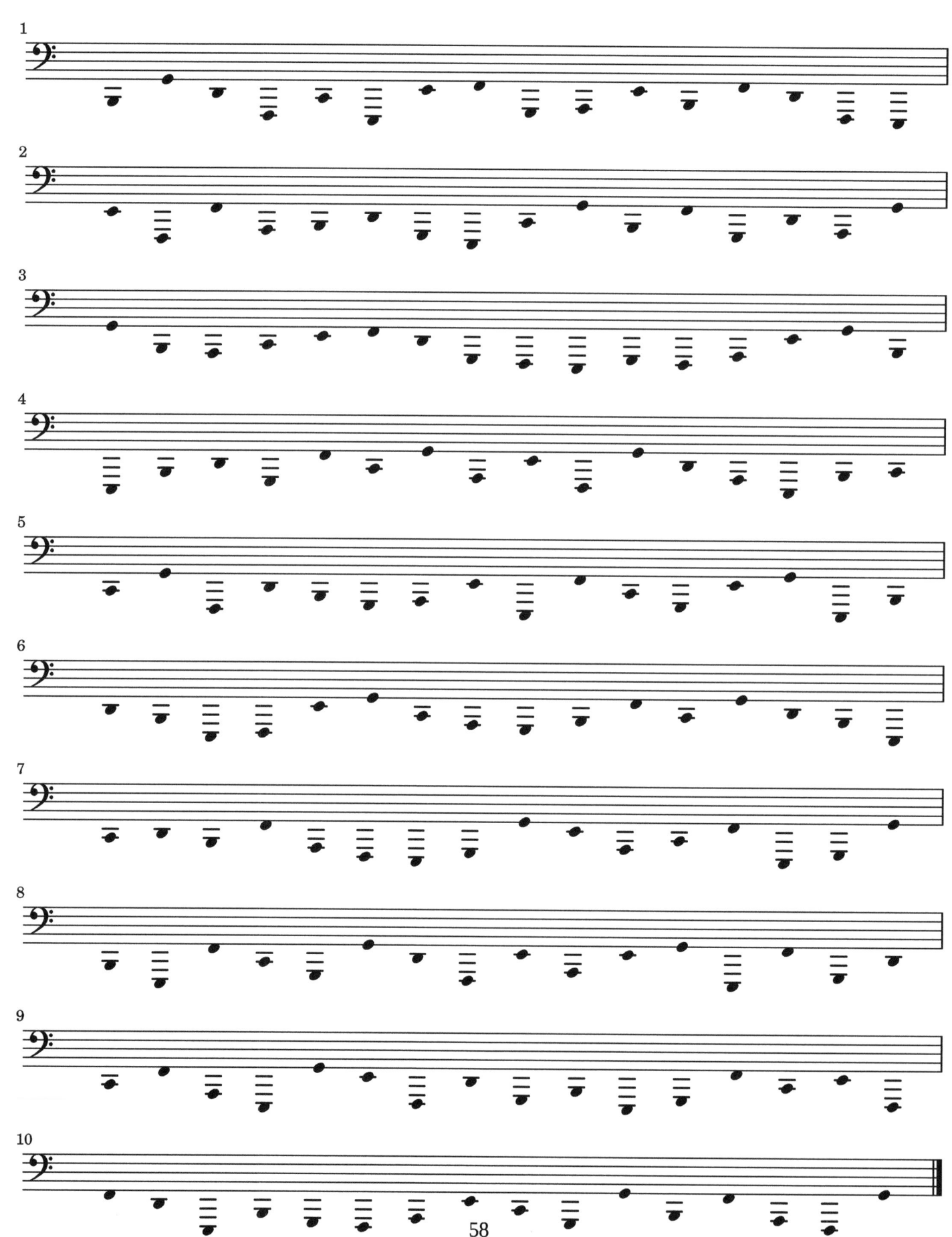

Below the Staff - Diatonic
Exercise 12 - Fourth Ledger Line

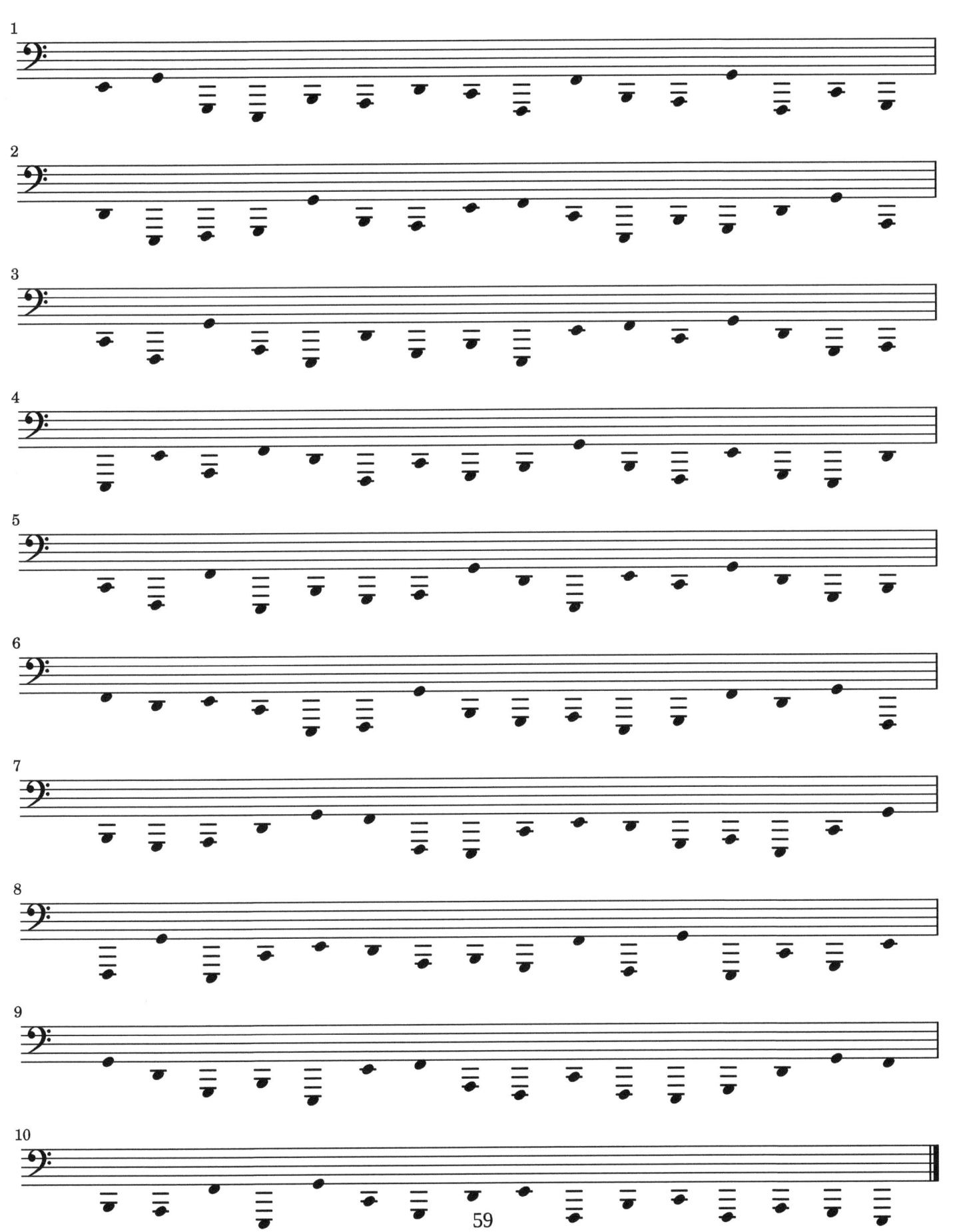

Chapter 6:

Below the Staff Chromatic

Exercise Ranges:

Below the Staff - Chromatic
Exercise 1 - First Ledger Line

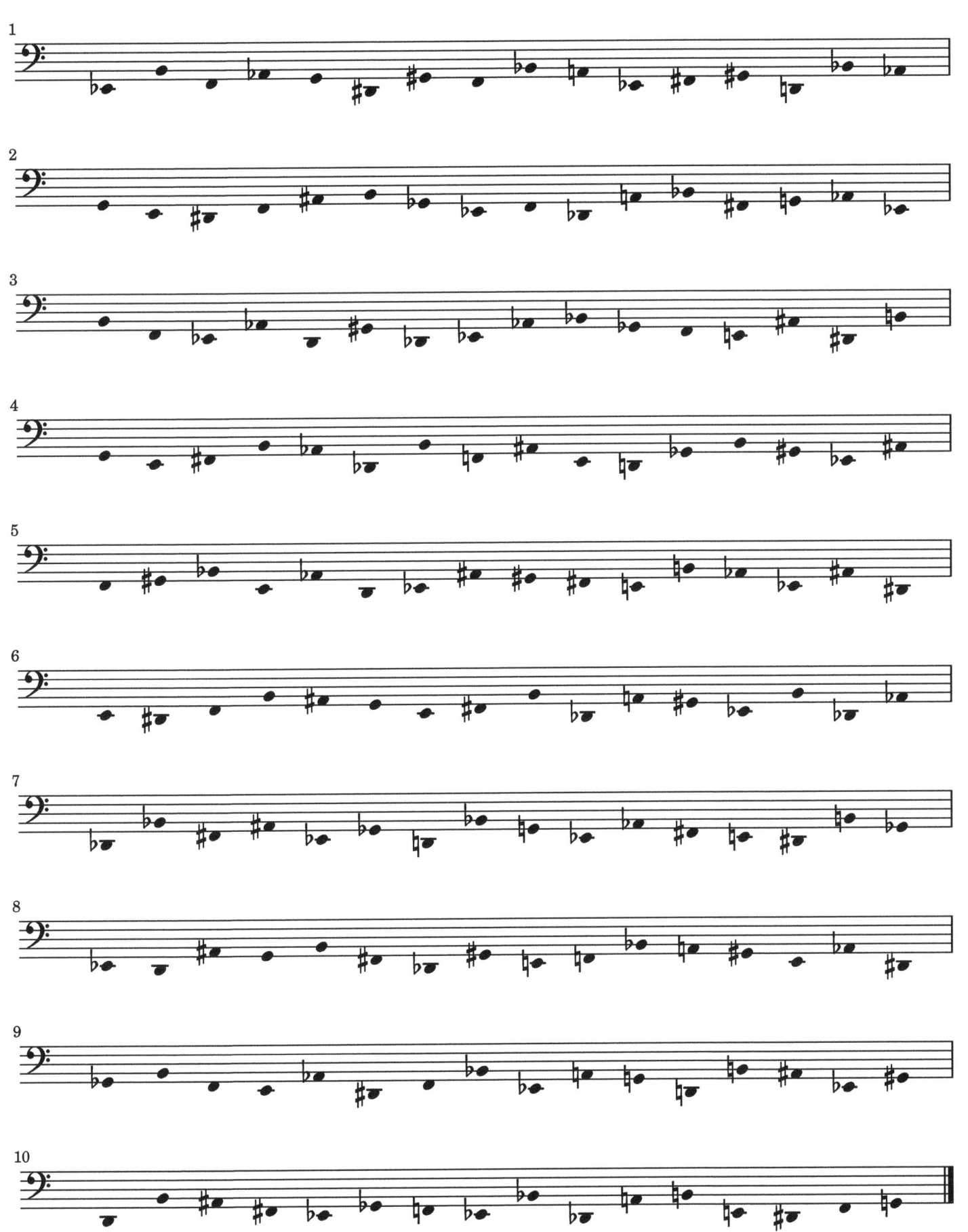

Below the Staff - Chromatic
Exercise 2 - First Ledger Line

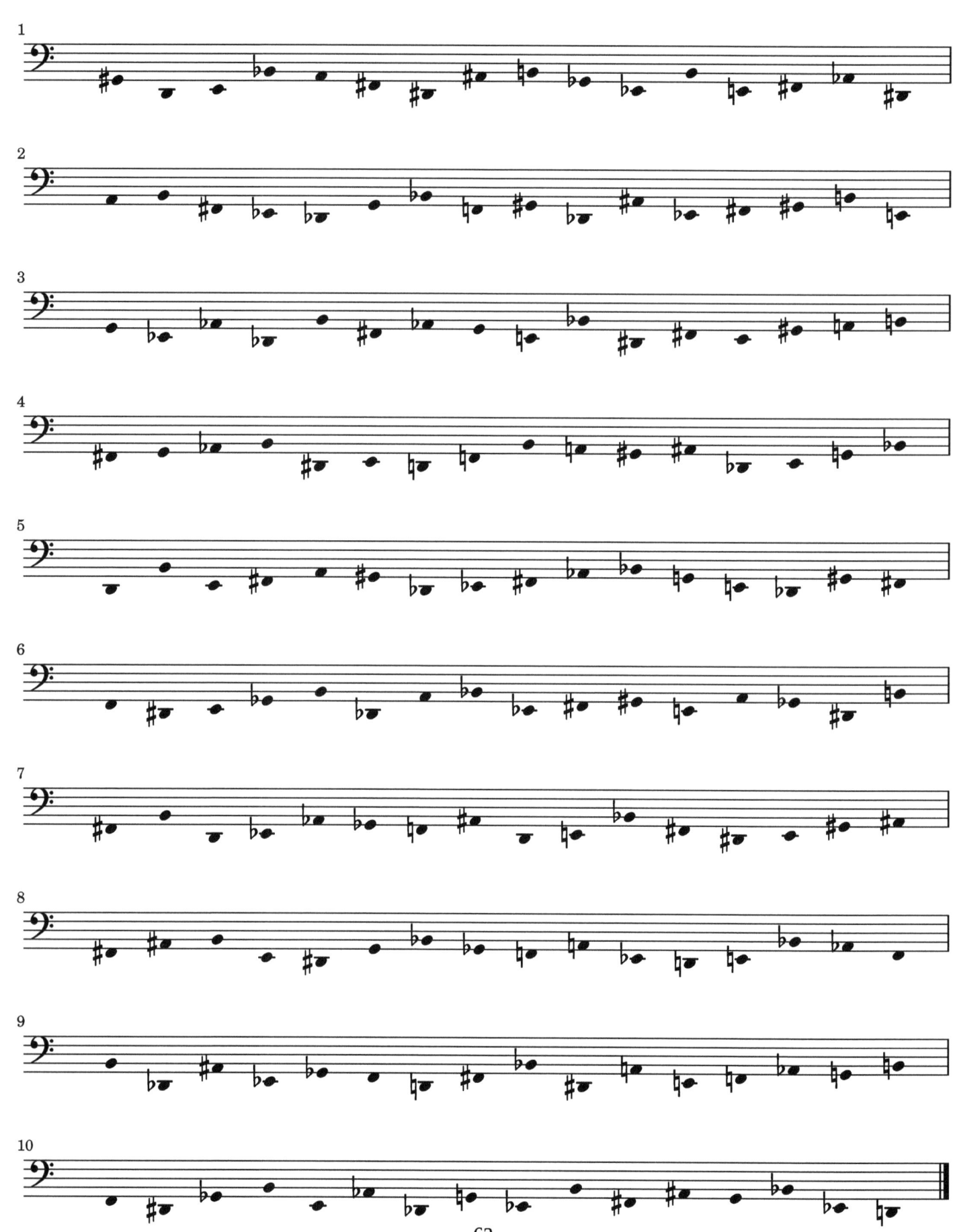

Below the Staff - Chromatic

Exercise 3 - First Ledger Line - Including B#, C♭, E#, F♭

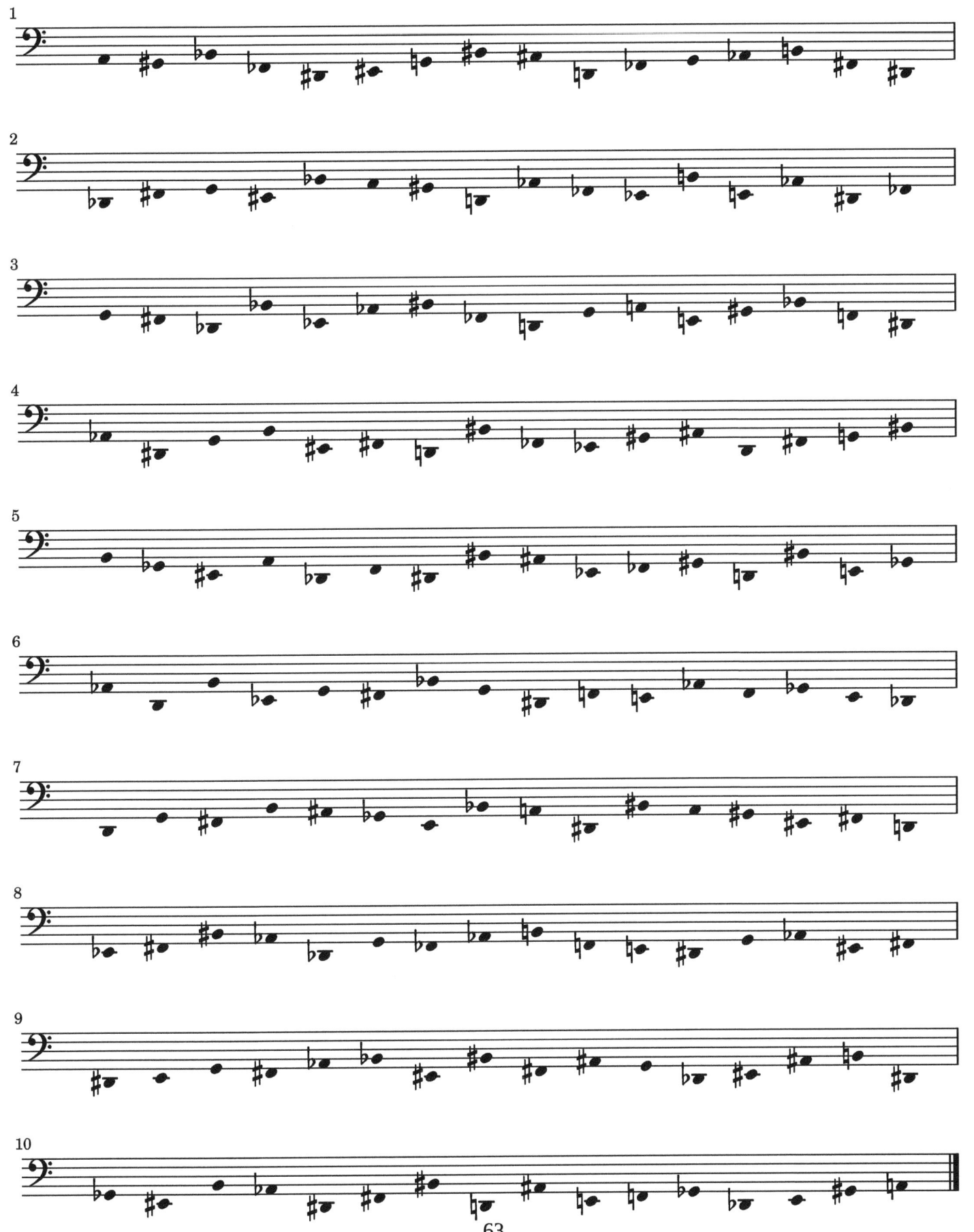

Below the Staff - Chromatic

Exercise 4 - Second Ledger Line

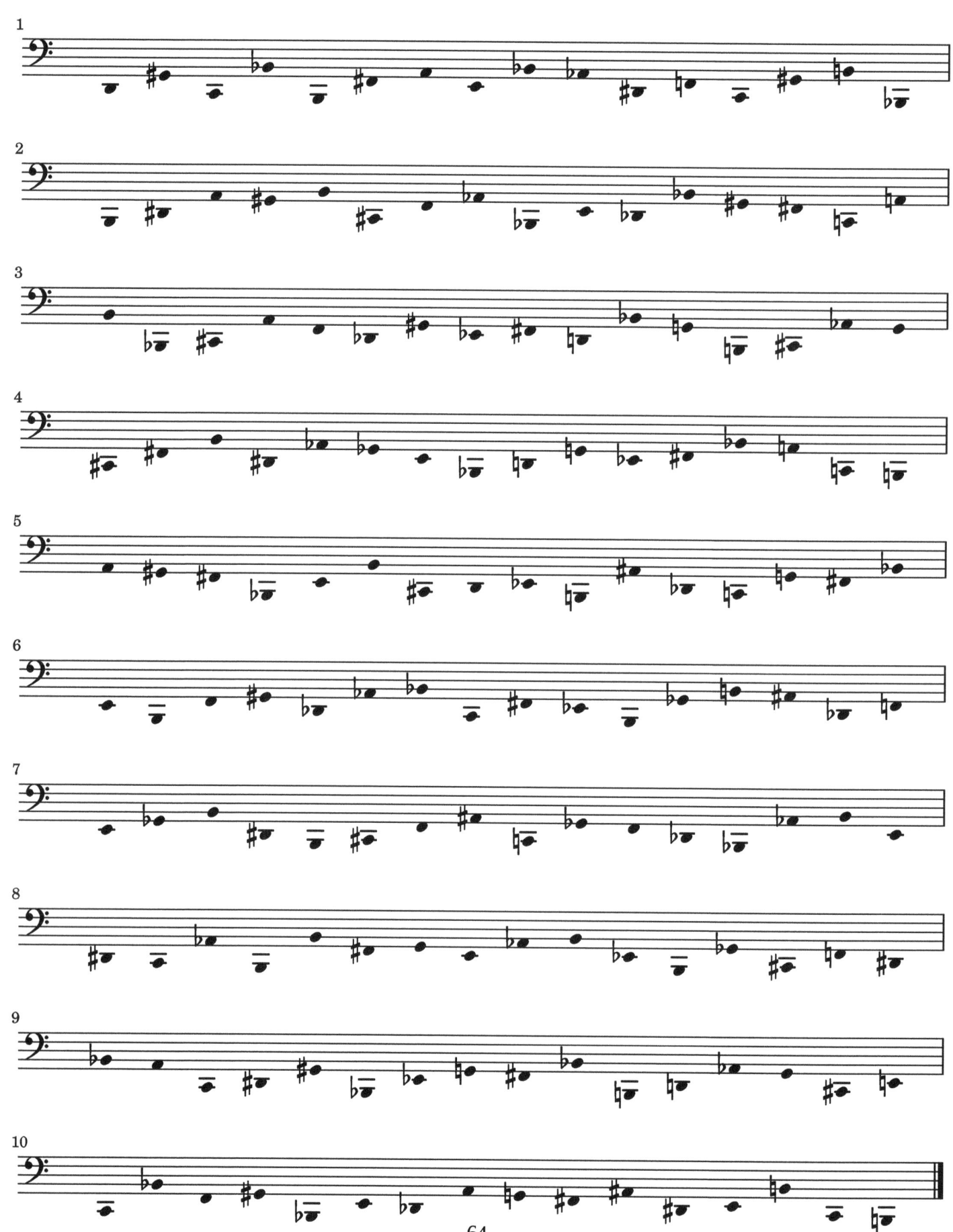

Below the Staff - Chromatic
Exercise 5 - Second Ledger Line

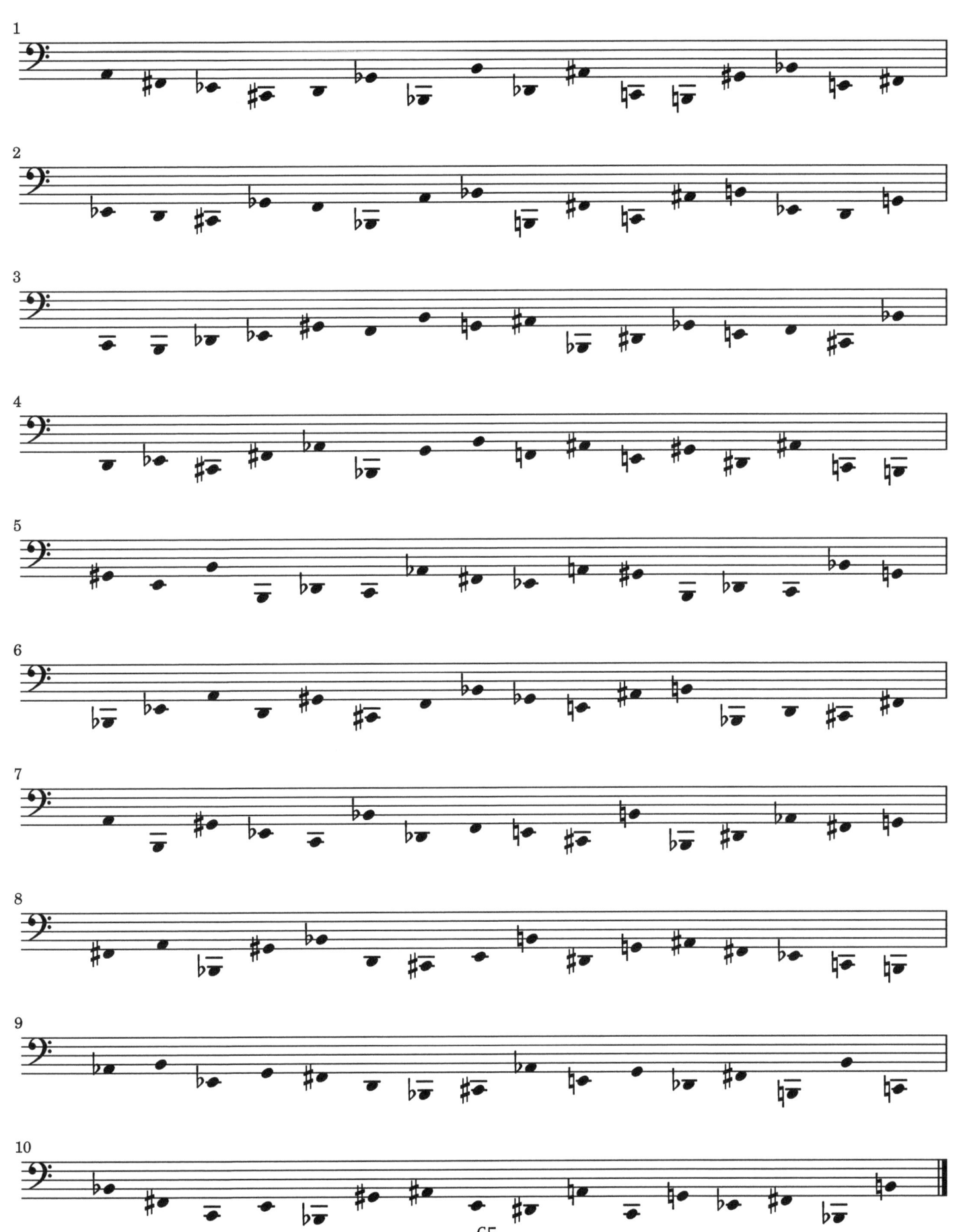

Below the Staff - Chromatic
Exercise 6 - Second Ledger Line - Including B♯, C♭, E♯, F♭

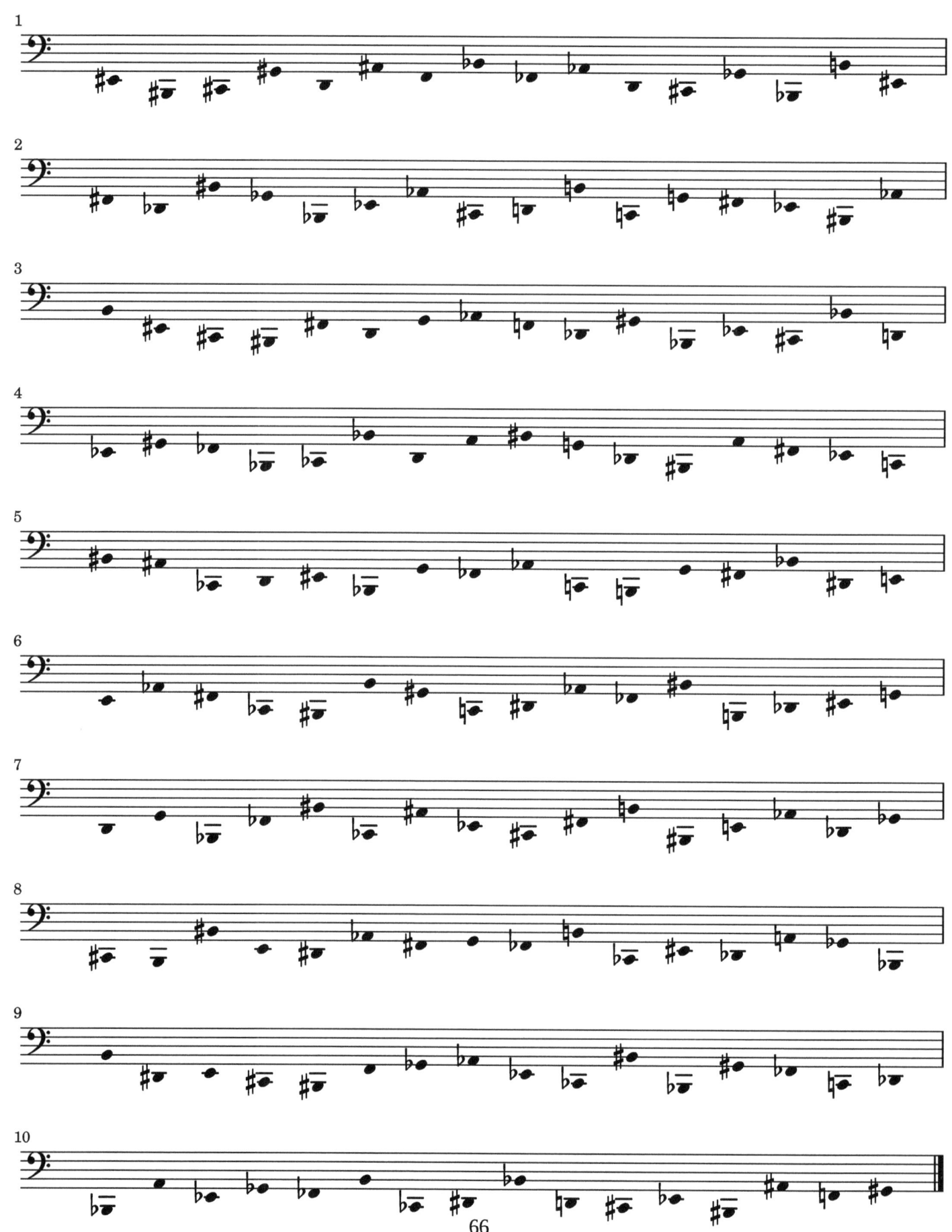

Below the Staff - Chromatic
Exercise 7 - Third Ledger Line

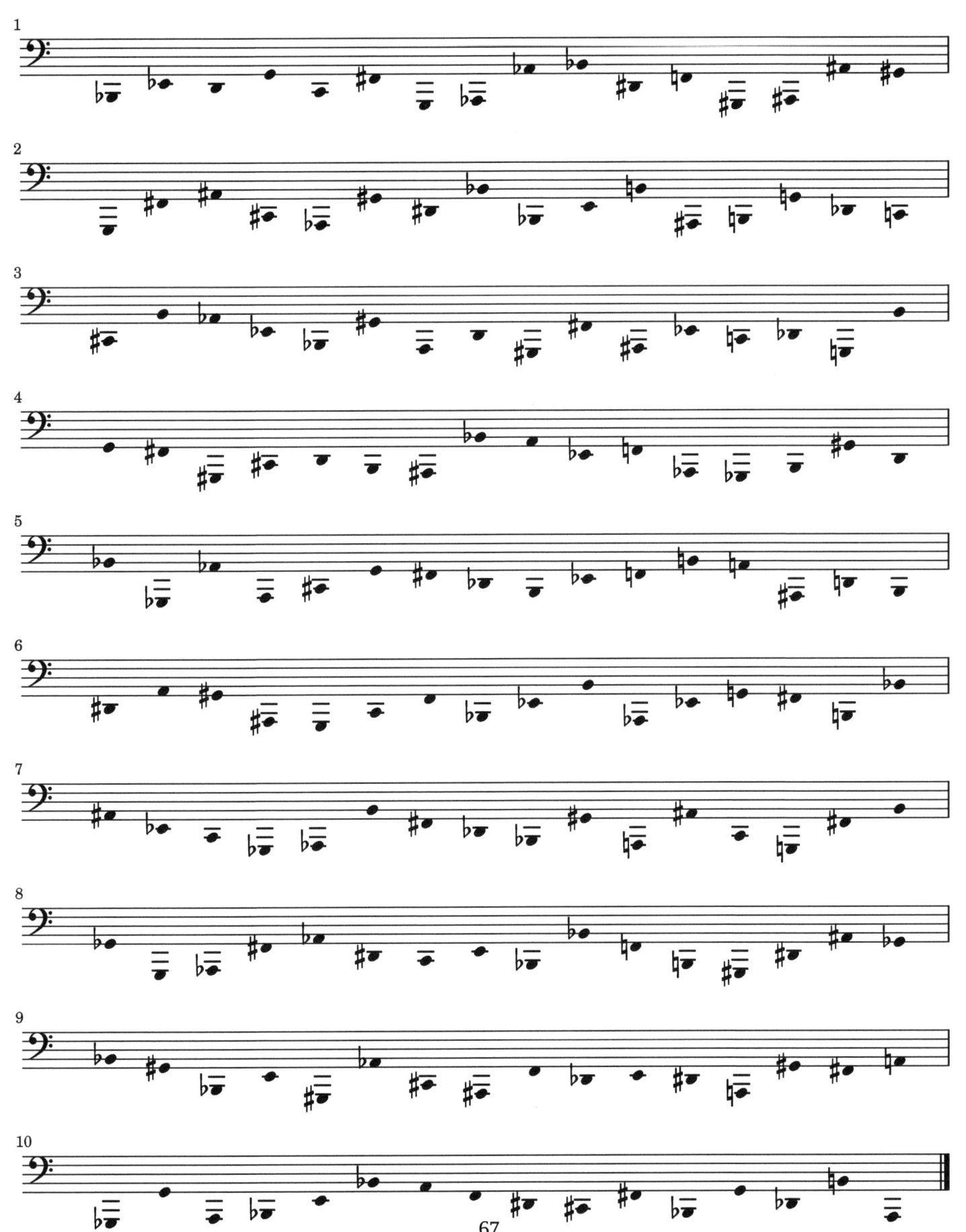

Below the Staff - Chromatic

Exercise 8 - Third Ledger Line

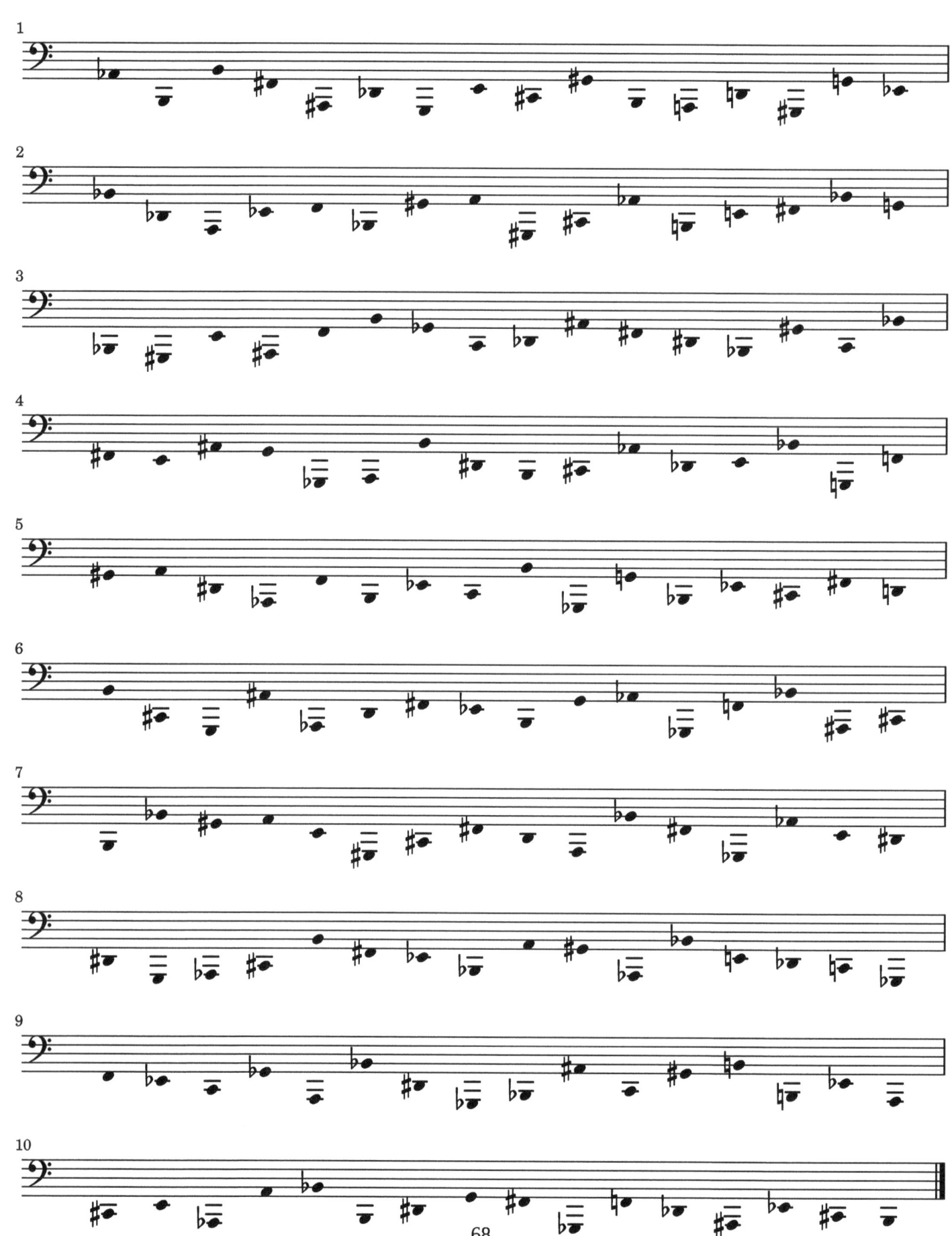

Below the Staff - Chromatic

Exercise 9 - Third Ledger Line - Including B#, C♭, E#, F♭

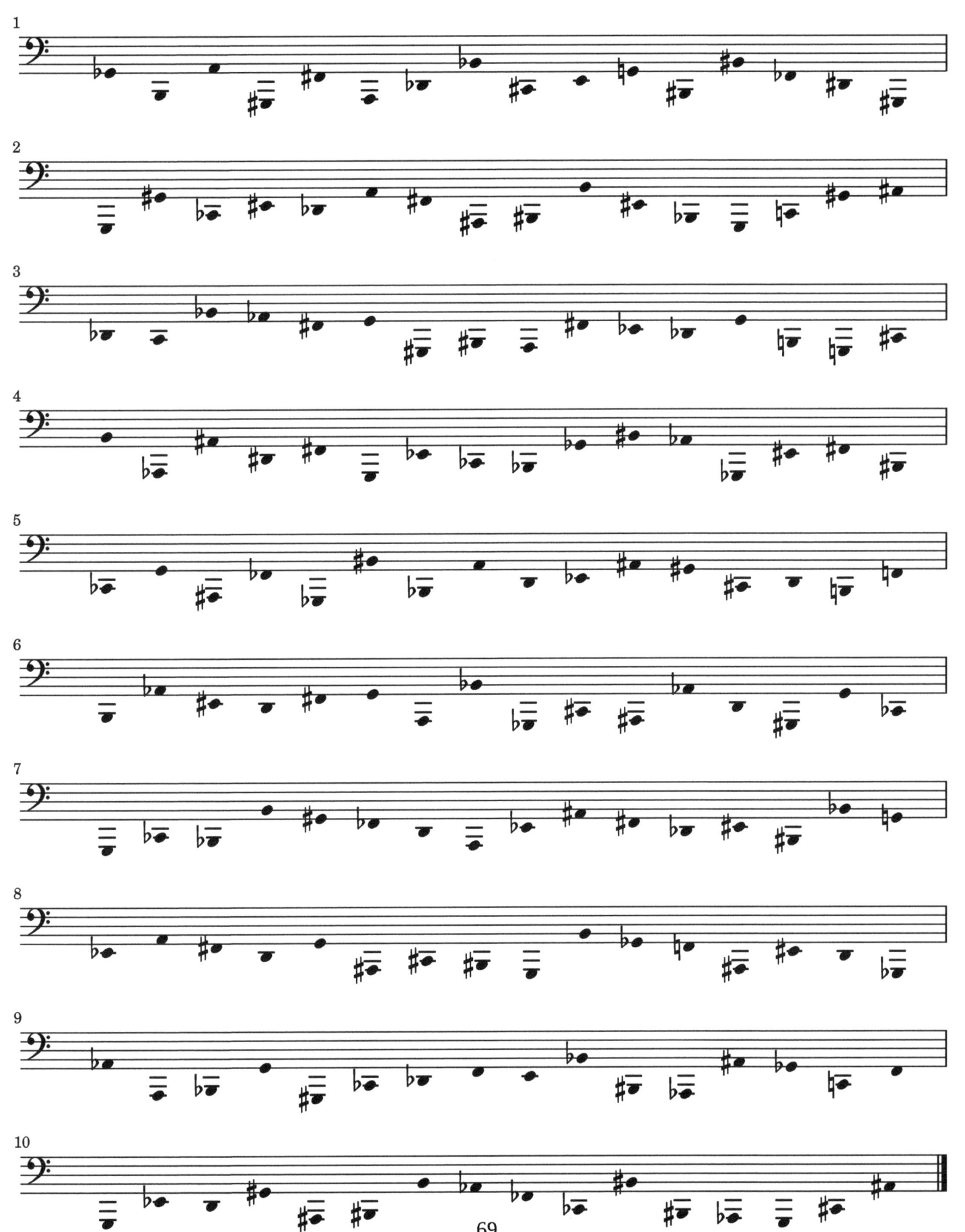

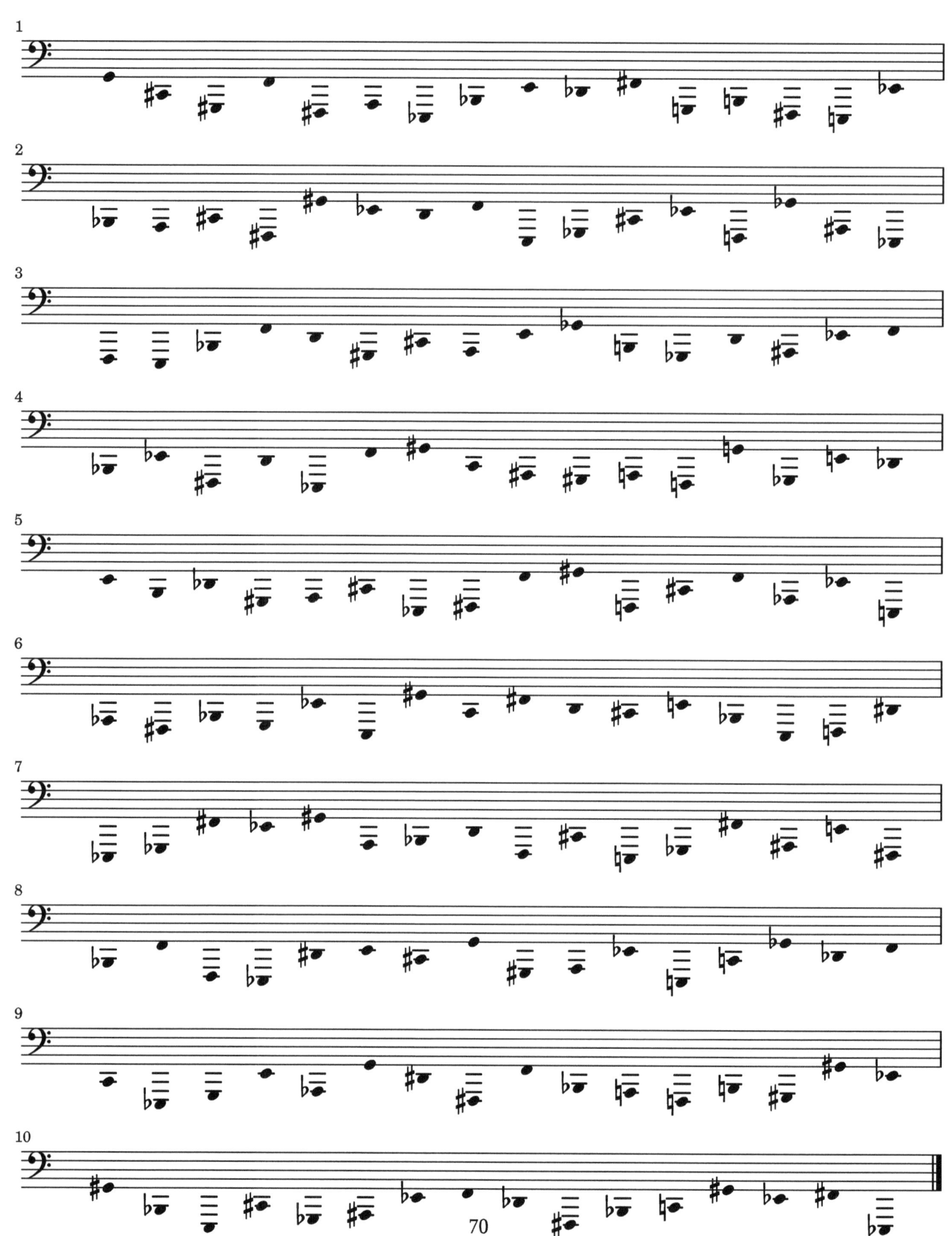

Below the Staff - Chromatic
Exercise 11 - Fourth Ledger Line

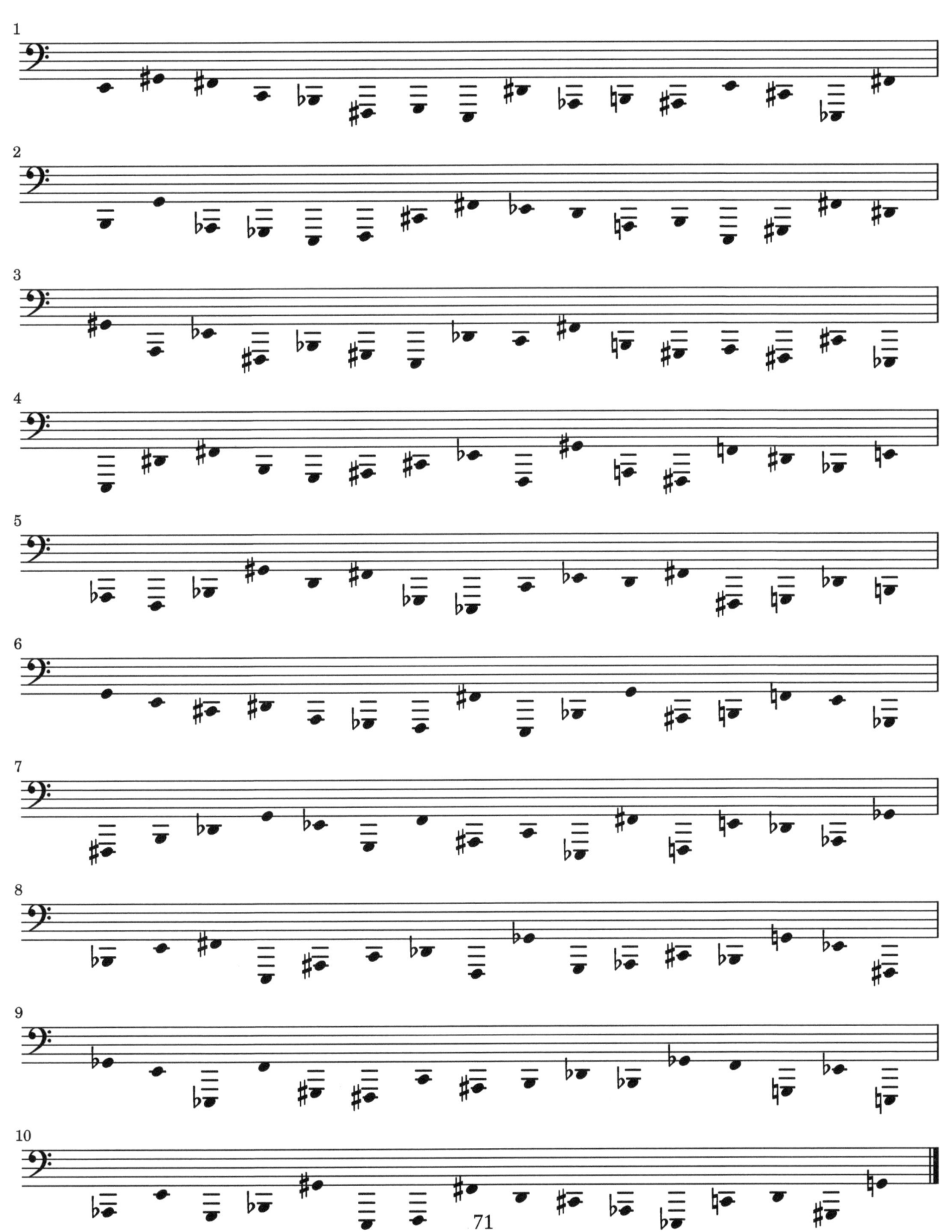

Below the Staff - Chromatic
Exercise 12 - Fourth Ledger Line - Including B#, C♭, E#, F♭

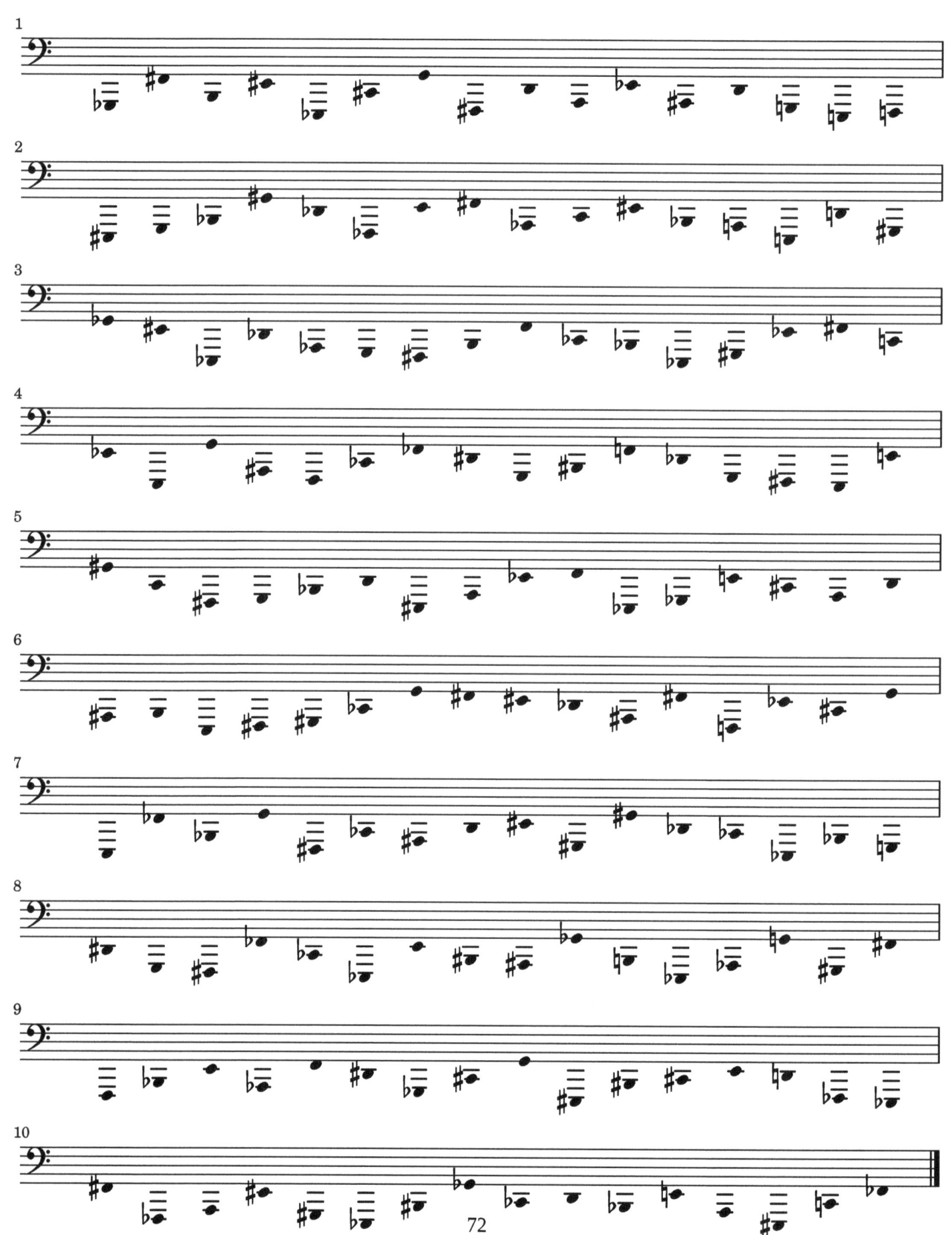

Chapter 7:

On and Above the Staff Diatonic

Exercise Ranges:

On and Above the Staff - Diatonic

Exercise 1 - First Ledger Line

On and Above the Staff - Diatonic

Exercise 2 - First Ledger Line

On and Above the Staff - Diatonic

Exercise 3 - First Ledger Line

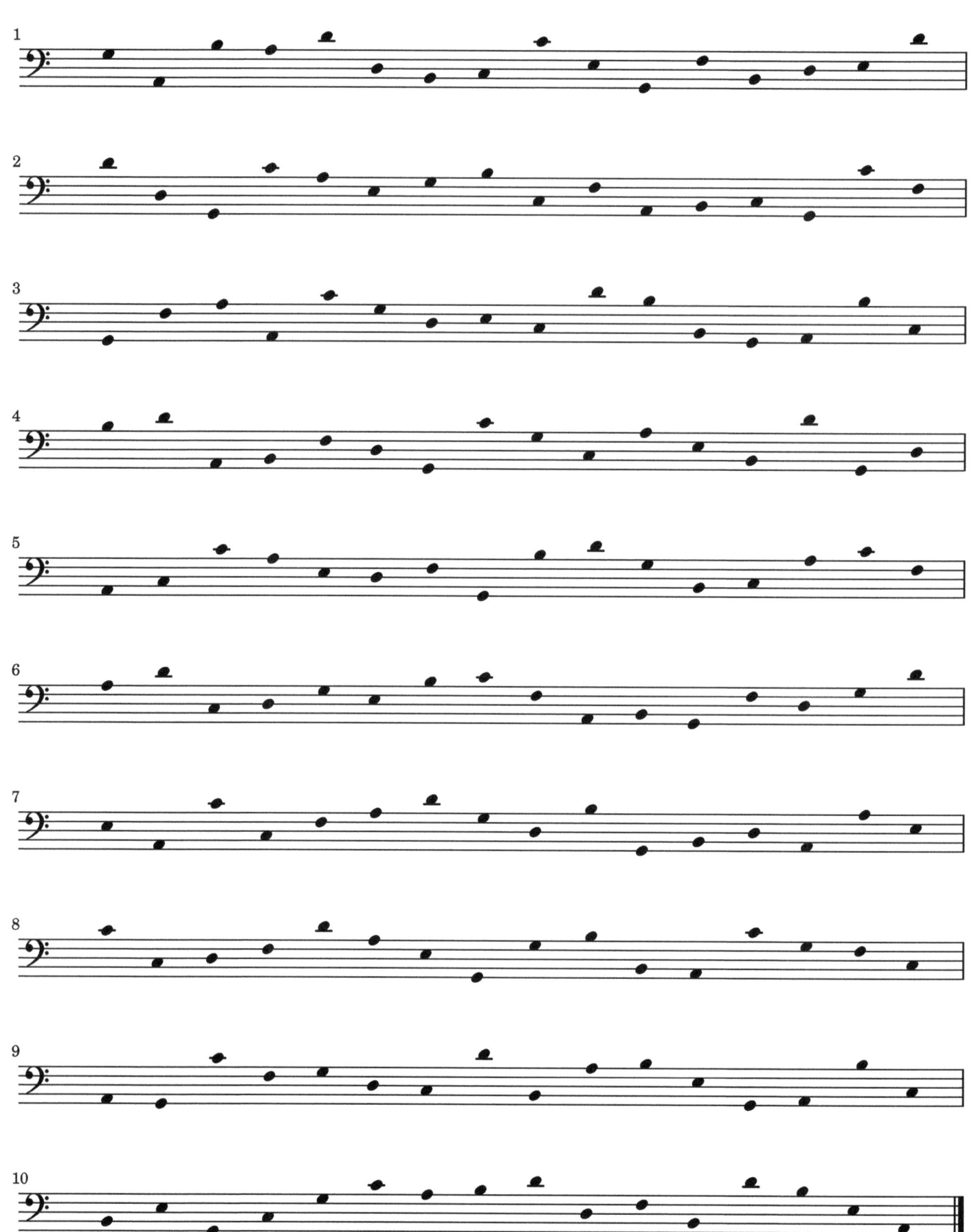

On and Above the Staff - Diatonic

Exercise 4 - Second Ledger Line

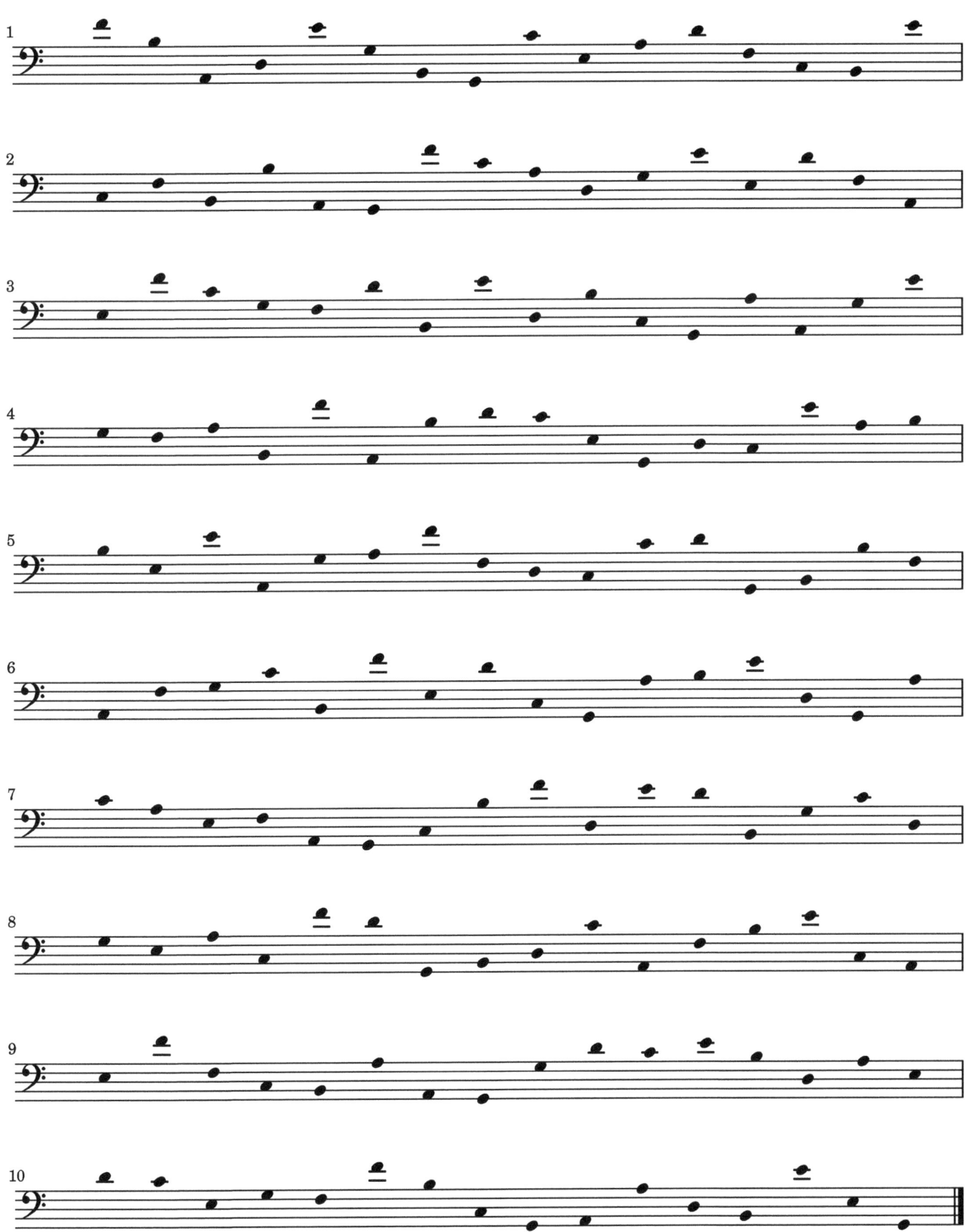

On and Above the Staff - Diatonic

Exercise 5 - Second Ledger Line

On and Above the Staff - Diatonic

Exercise 6 - Second Ledger Line

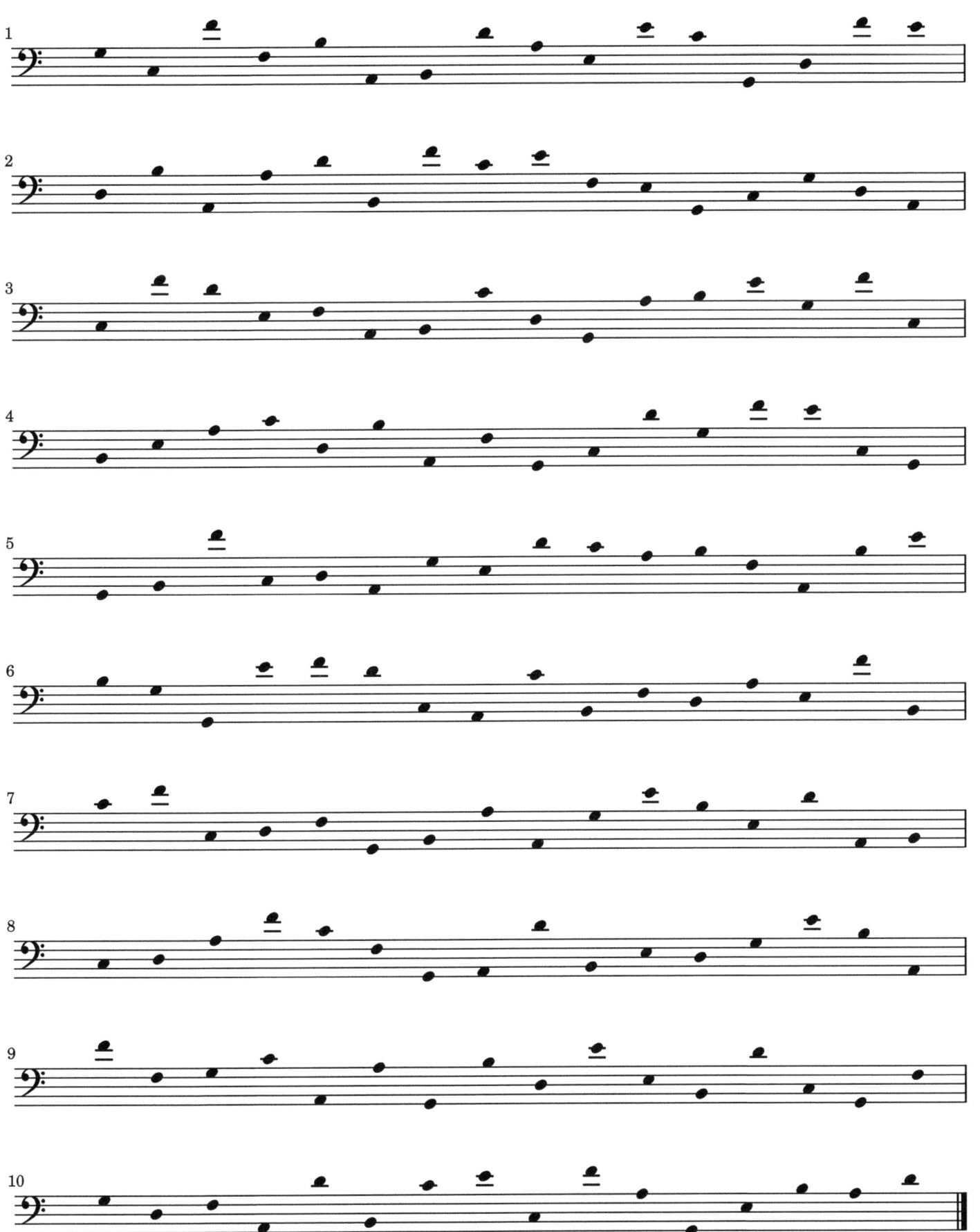

On and Above the Staff - Diatonic

Exercise 7 - Third Ledger Line

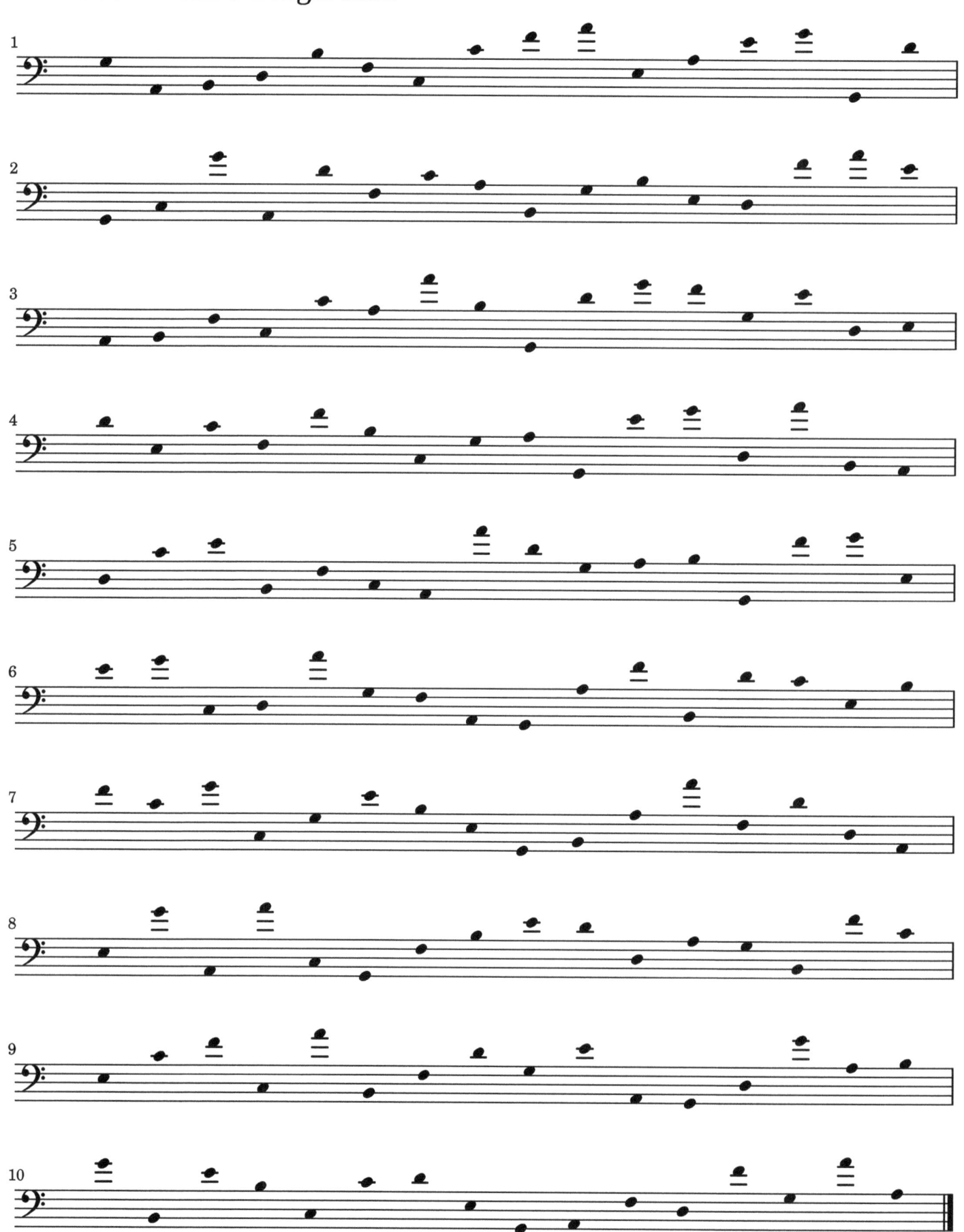

On and Above the Staff - Diatonic

Exercise 8 - Third Ledger Line

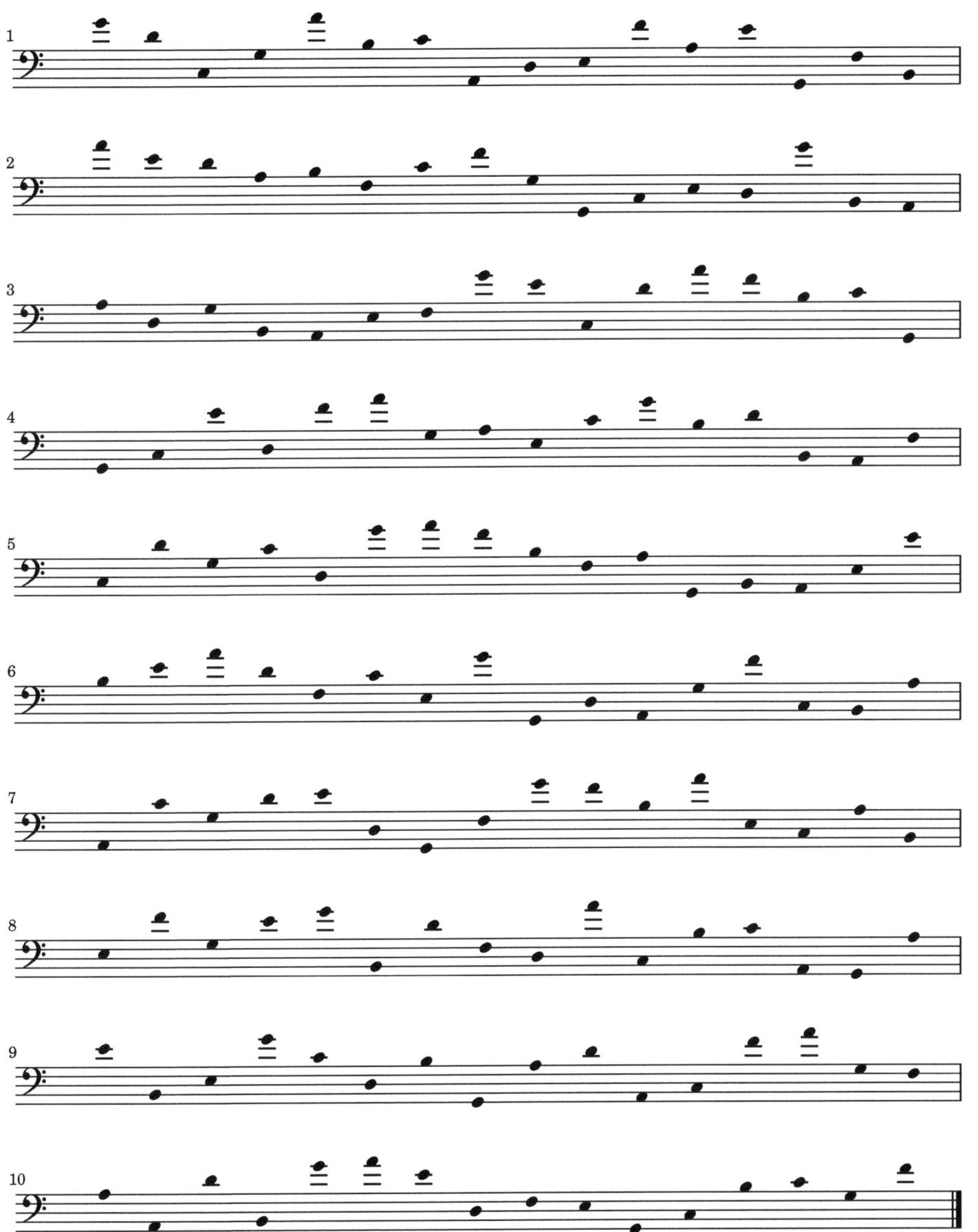

On and Above the Staff - Diatonic

Exercise 9 - Third Ledger Line

On and Above the Staff - Diatonic

Exercise 10 - Fourth Ledger Line

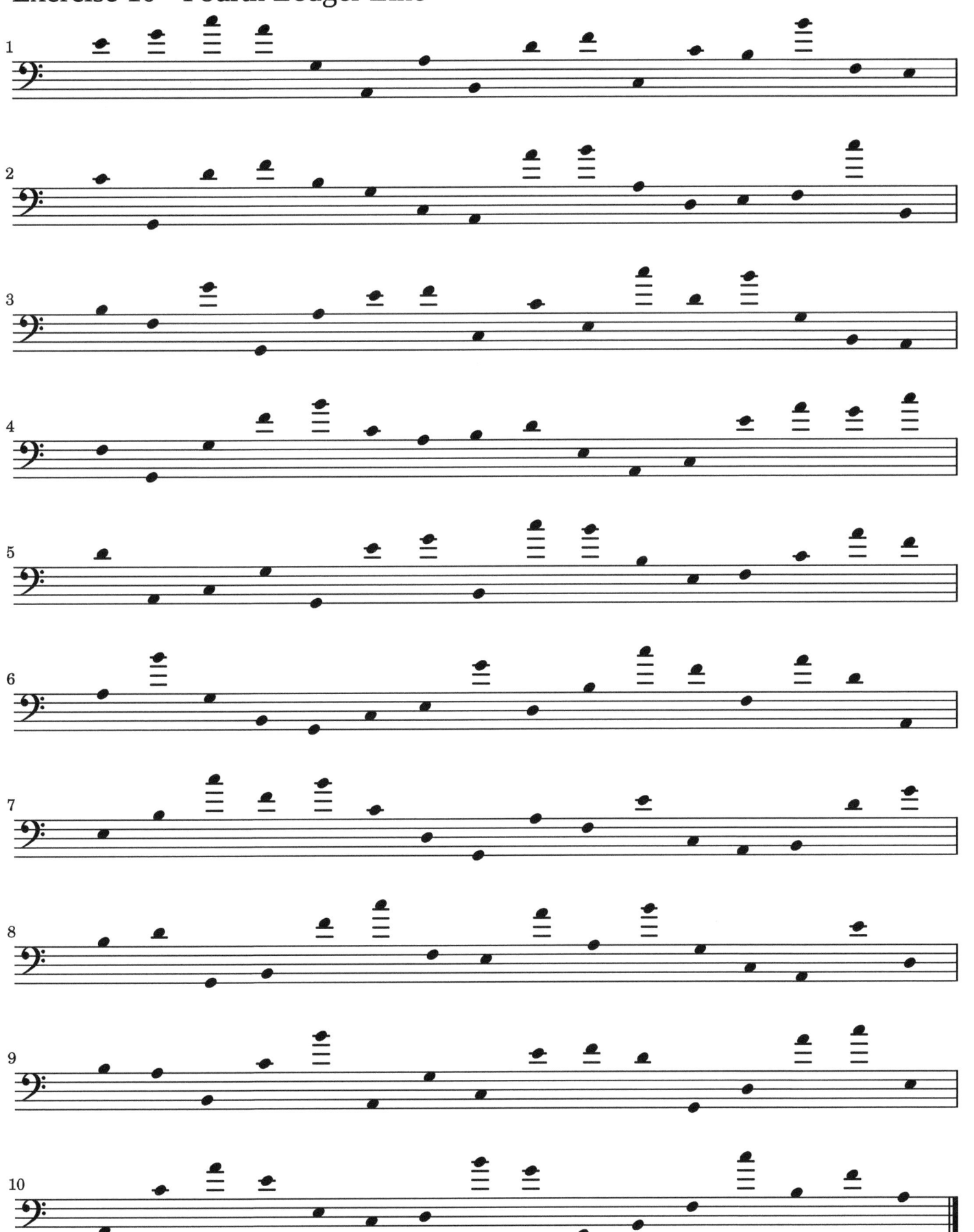

On and Above the Staff - Diatonic

Exercise 11 - Fourth Ledger Line

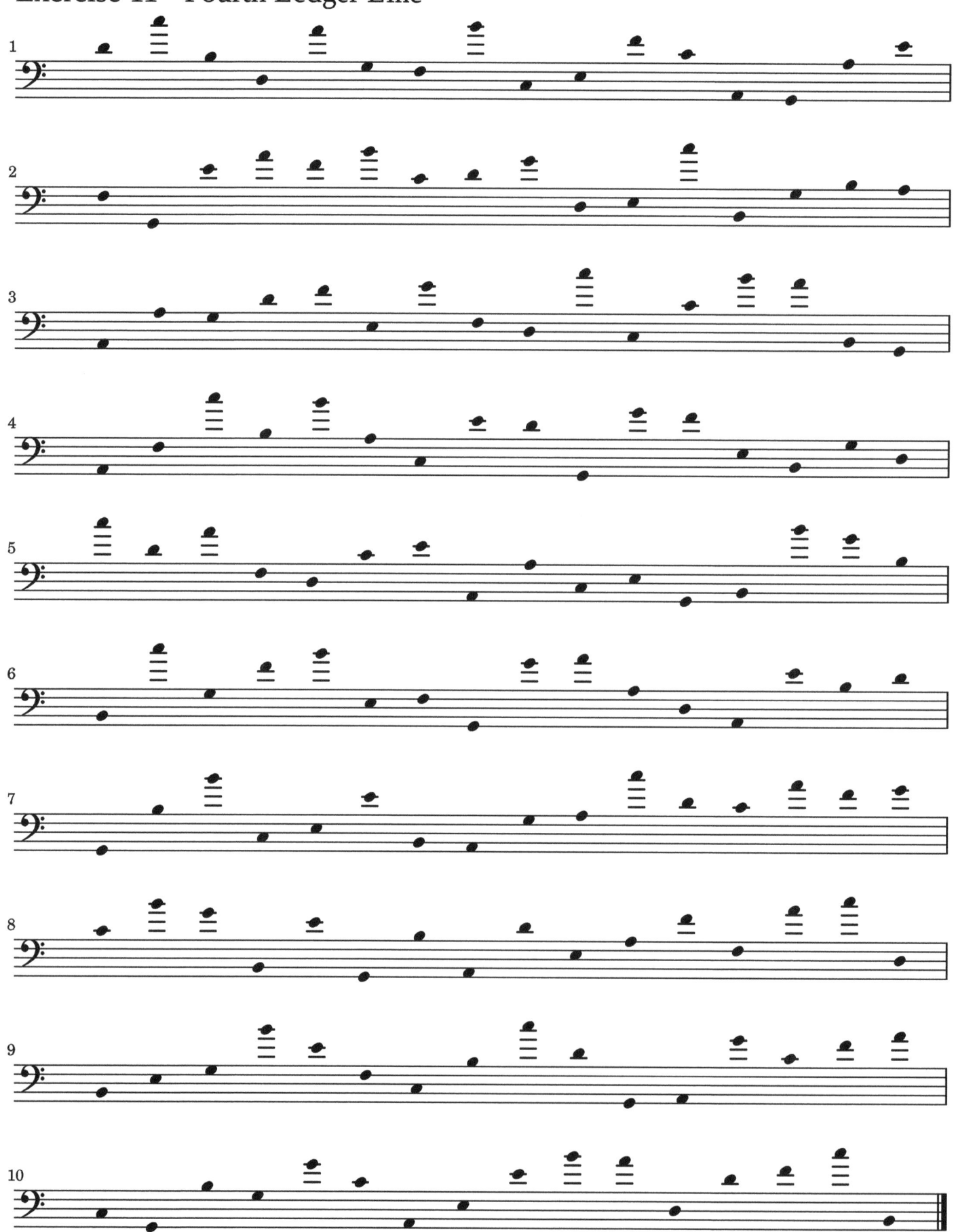

On and Above the Staff - Diatonic

Exercise 12 - Fourth Ledger Line

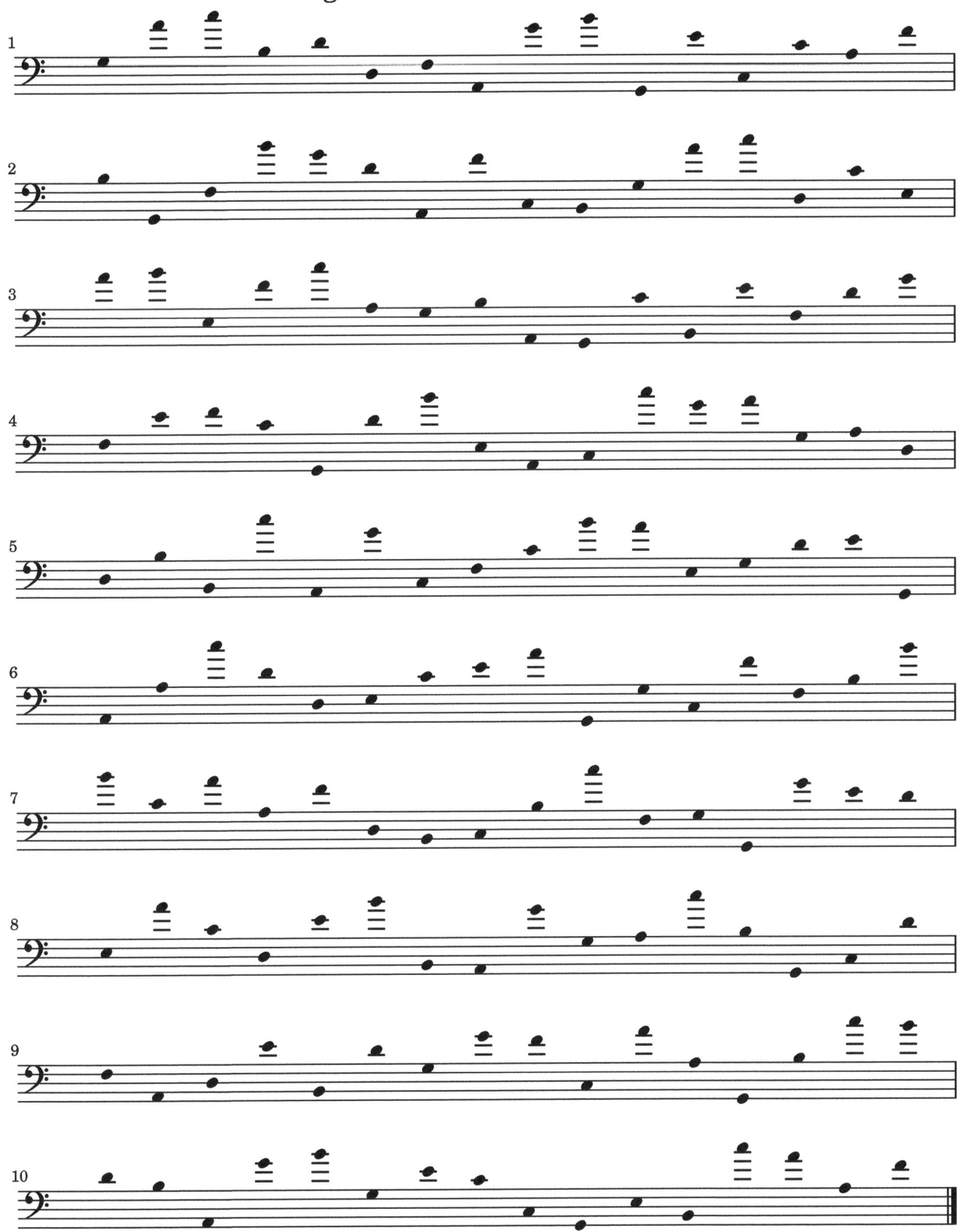

Chapter 8:

On and Above the Staff Chromatic

Exercise Ranges:

On and Above the Staff - Chromatic

Exercise 1 - First Ledger Line

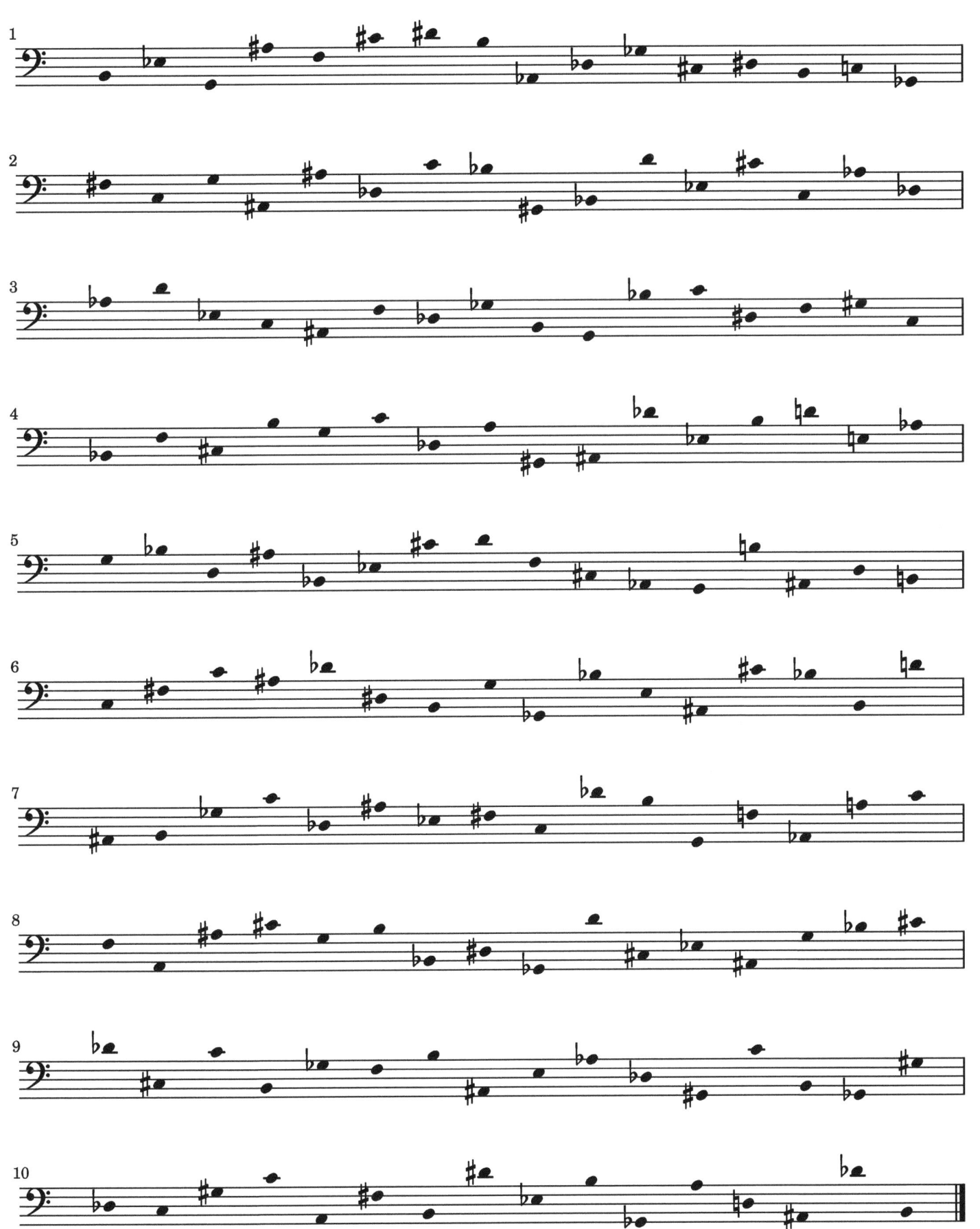

On and Above the Staff - Chromatic

Exercise 2 - First Ledger Line

On and Above the Staff - Chromatic

Exercise 3 - First Ledger Line - Including B♯, C♭, E♯, F♭

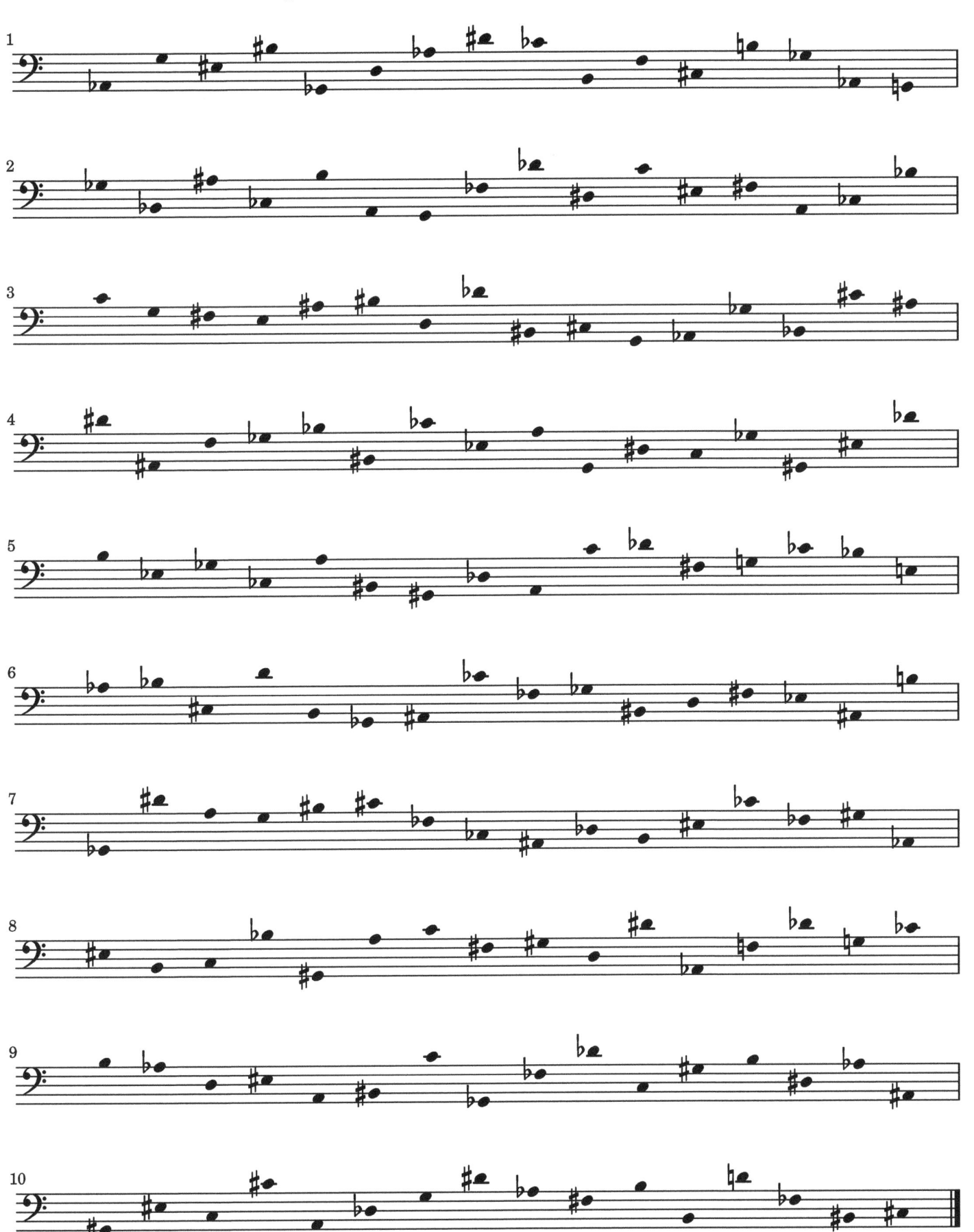

On and Above the Staff - Chromatic
Exercise 4 - Second Ledger Line

90

On and Above the Staff - Chromatic

Exercise 5 - Second Ledger Line

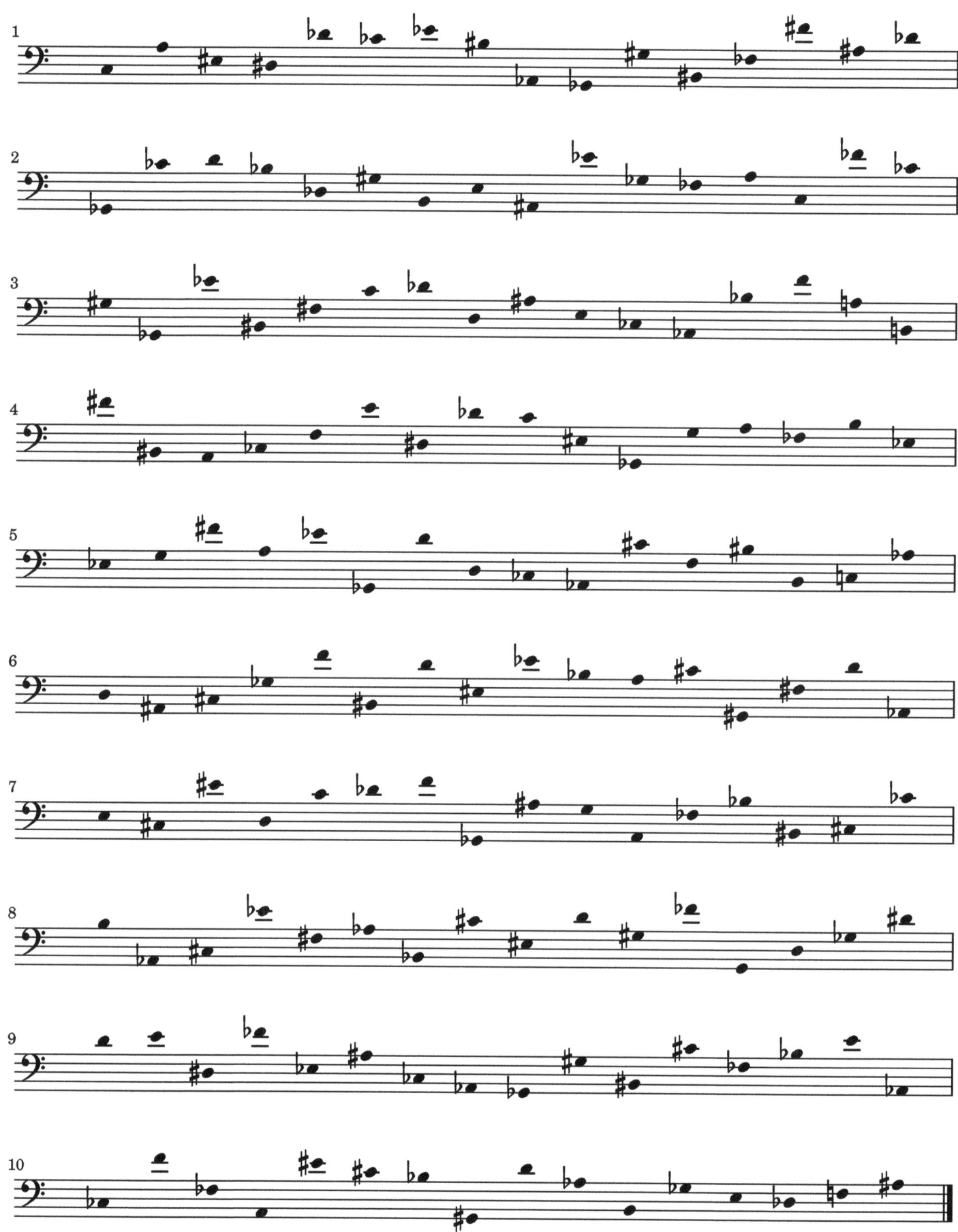

On and Above the Staff - Chromatic

Exercise 7 - Third Ledger Line

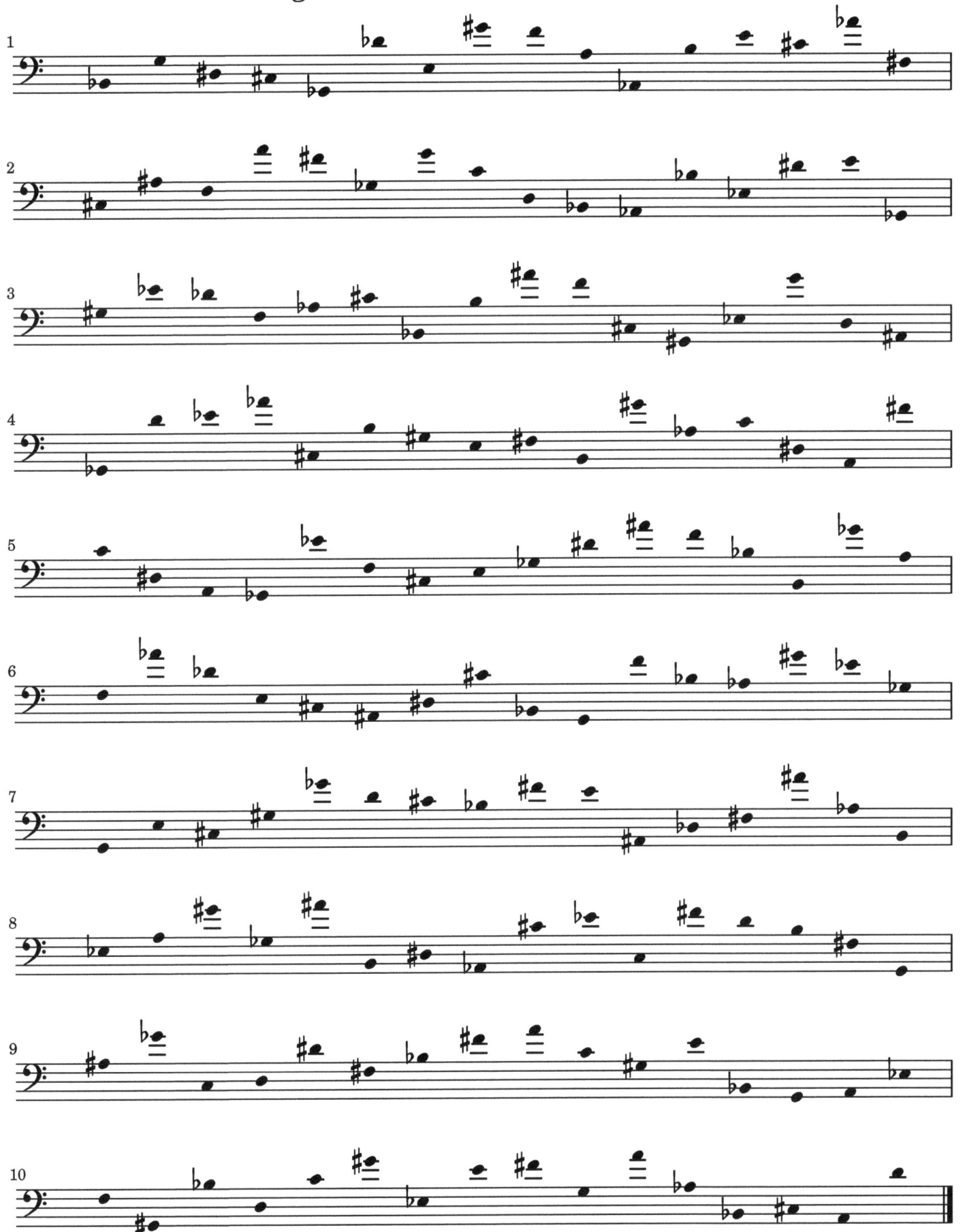

On and Above the Staff - Chromatic
Exercise 8 - Third Ledger Line

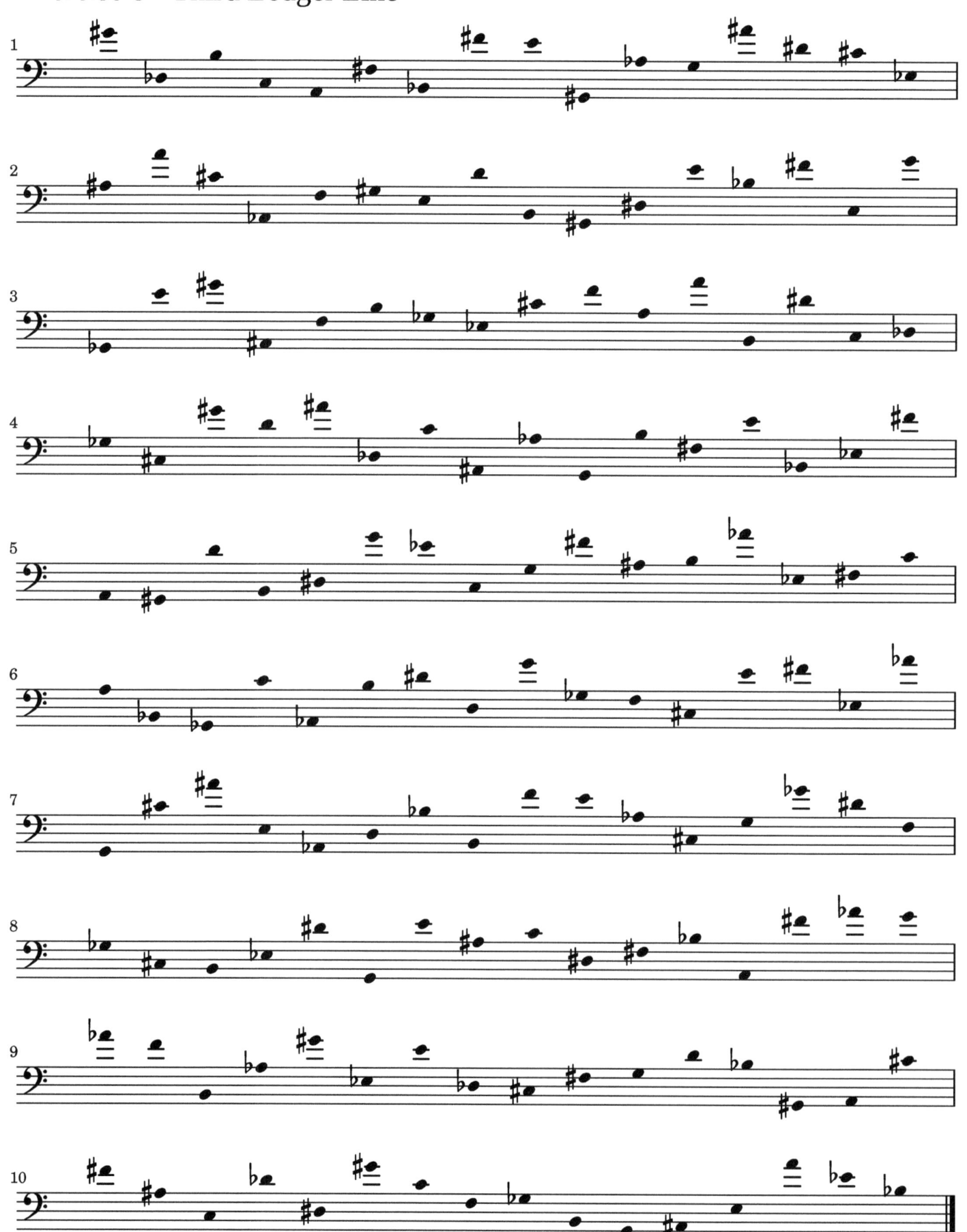

On and Above the Staff - Chromatic

Exercise 9 - Third Ledger Line - Including B#, C♭, E#, F♭

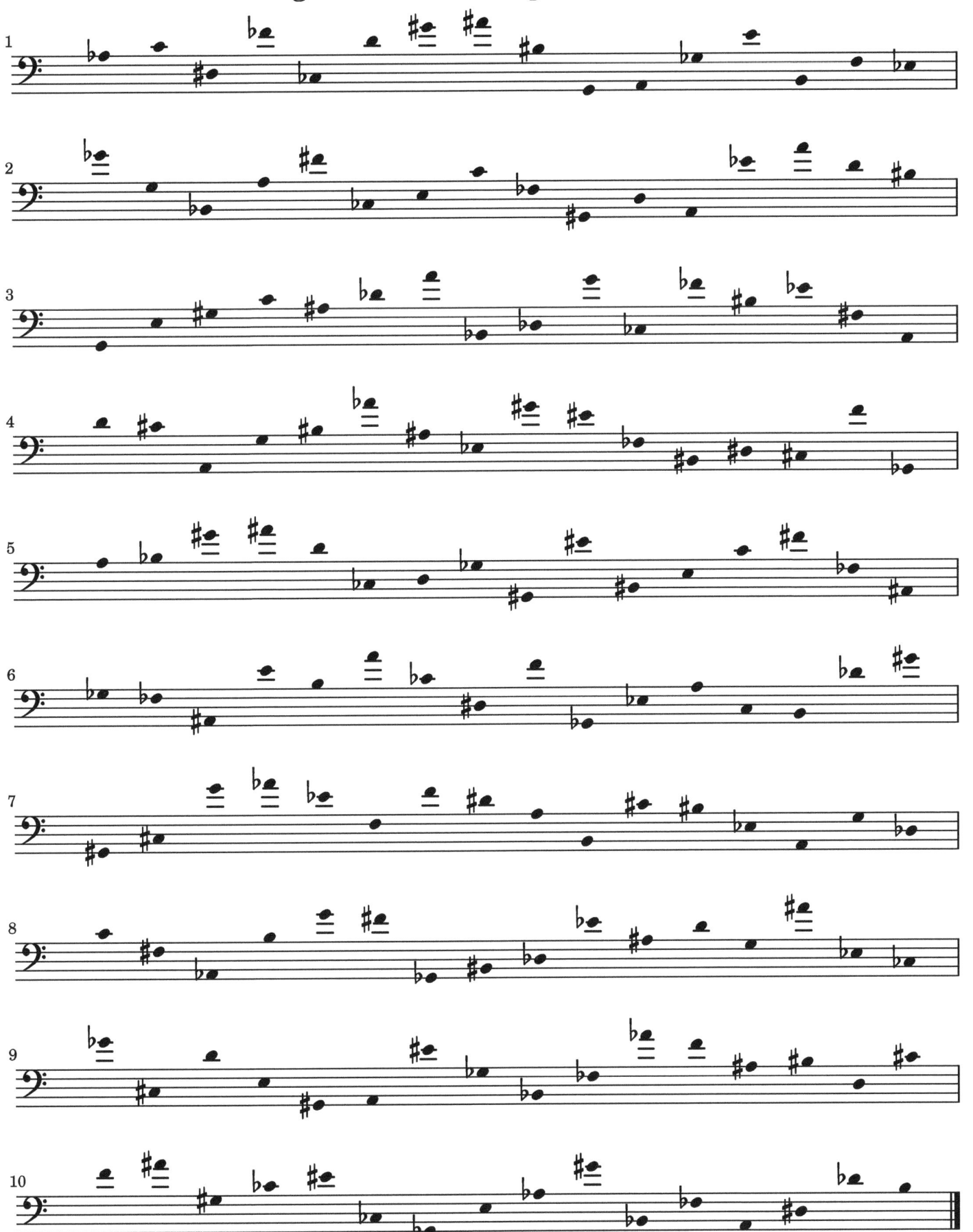

On and Above the Staff - Chromatic

Exercise 10 - Fourth Ledger Line

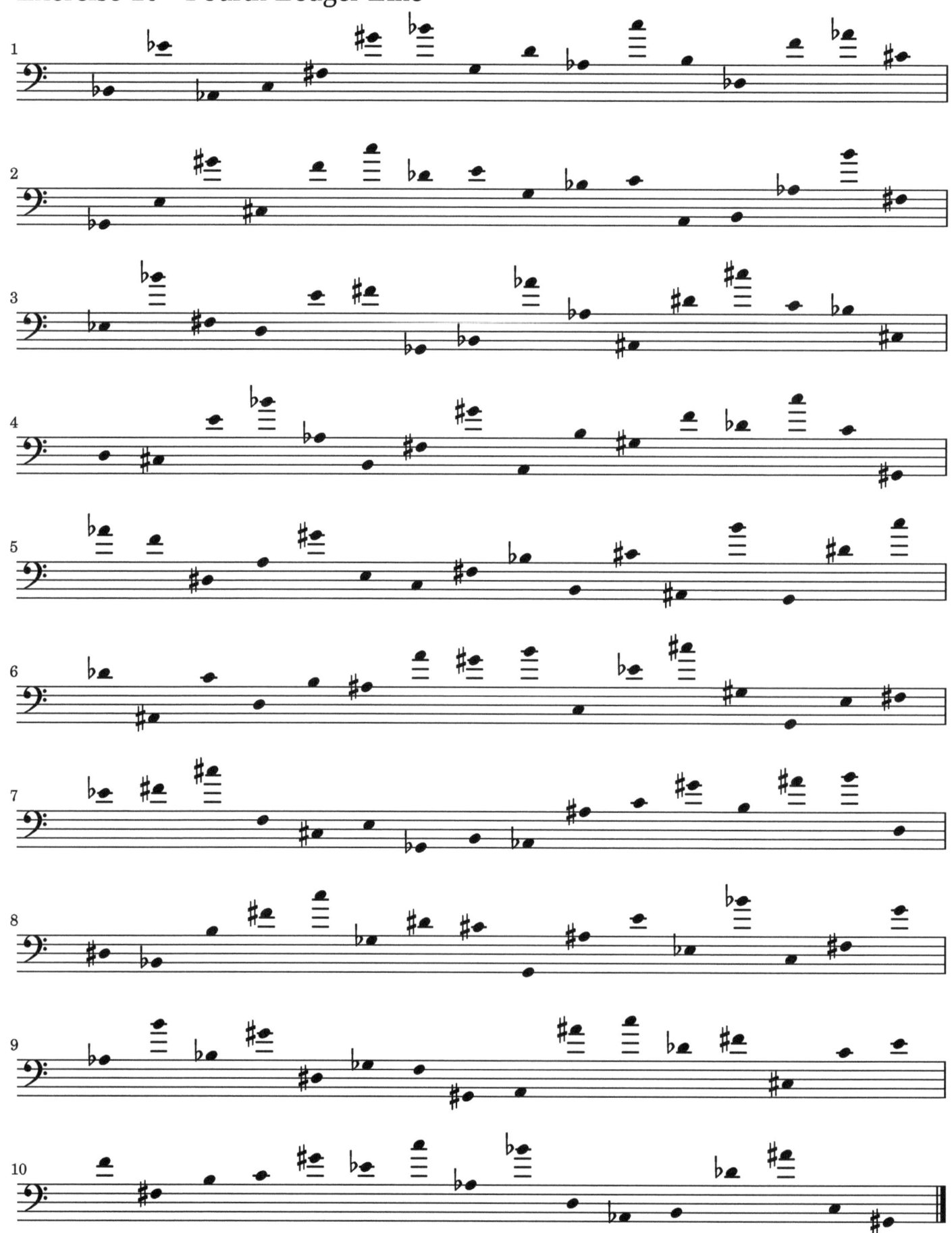

On and Above the Staff - Chromatic

Exercise 11 - Fourth Ledger Line

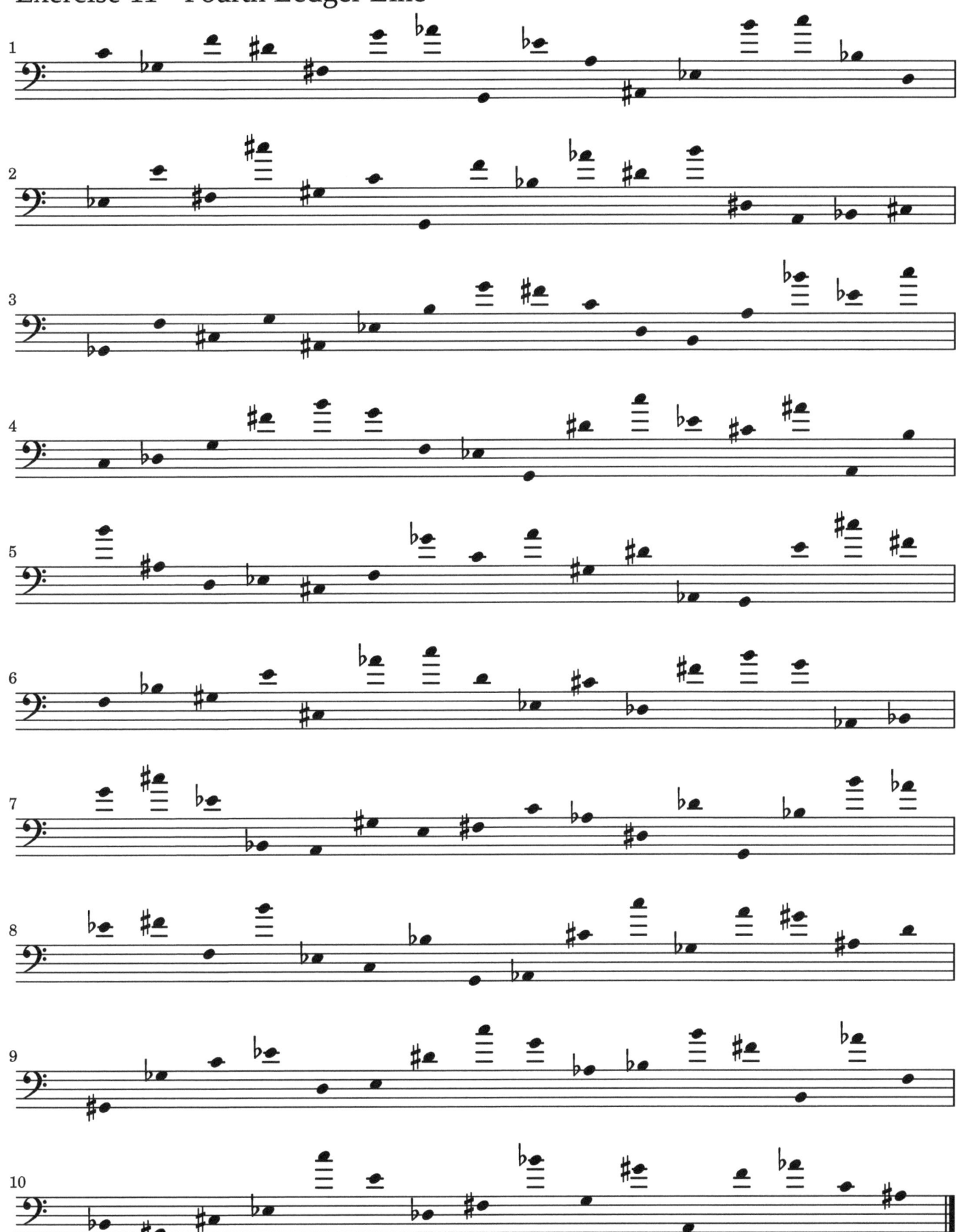

On and Above the Staff - Chromatic
Exercise 12 - Fourth Ledger Line - Including B#, C♭, E#, F♭

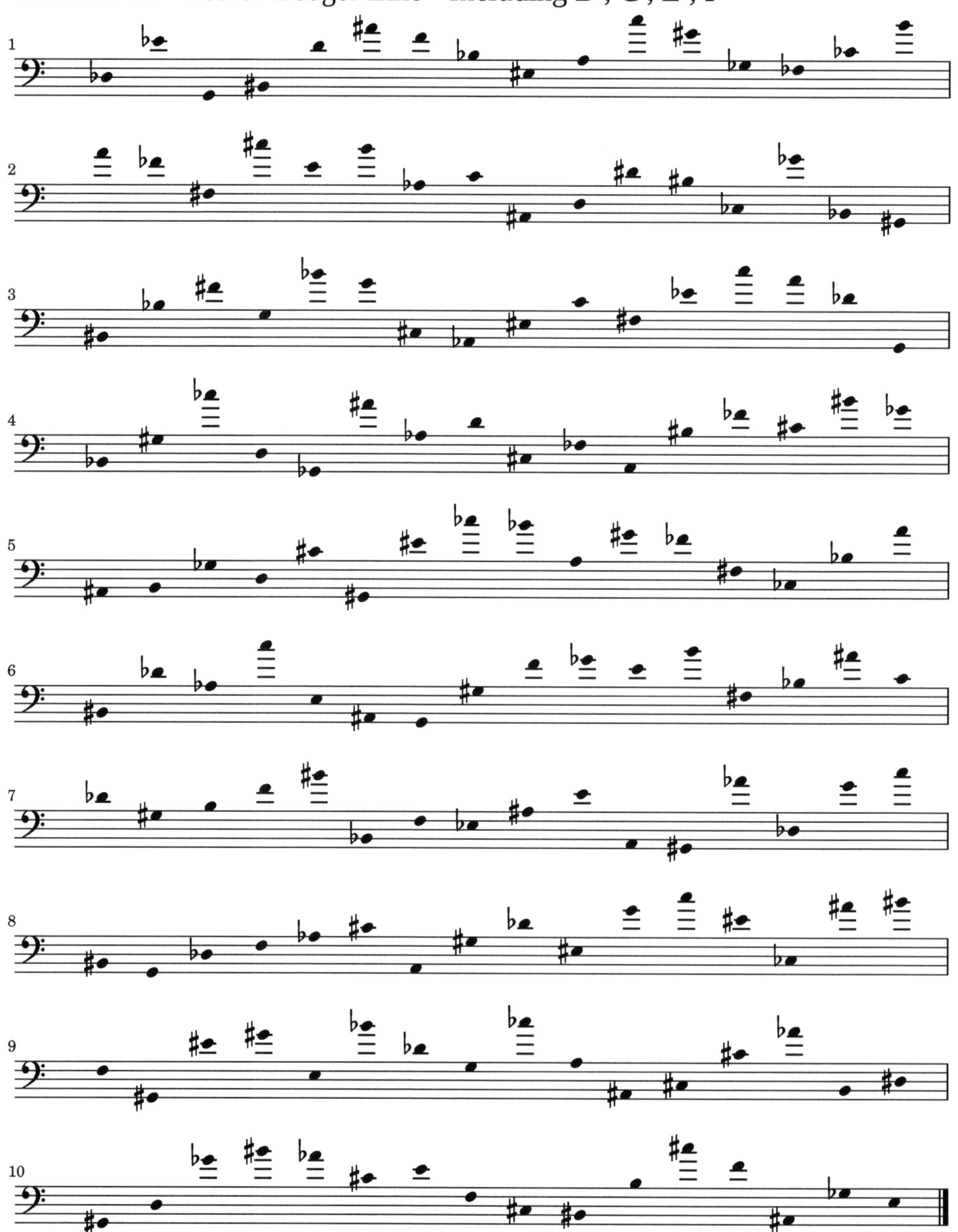

Chapter 9:

On and Below the Staff
Diatonic

Exercise Ranges:

On and Below the Staff - Diatonic

Exercise 1 - First Ledger Line

On and Below the Staff - Diatonic

Exercise 2 - First Ledger Line

On and Below the Staff - Diatonic
Exercise 3 - First Ledger Line

On and Below the Staff - Diatonic

Exercise 4 - Second Ledger Line

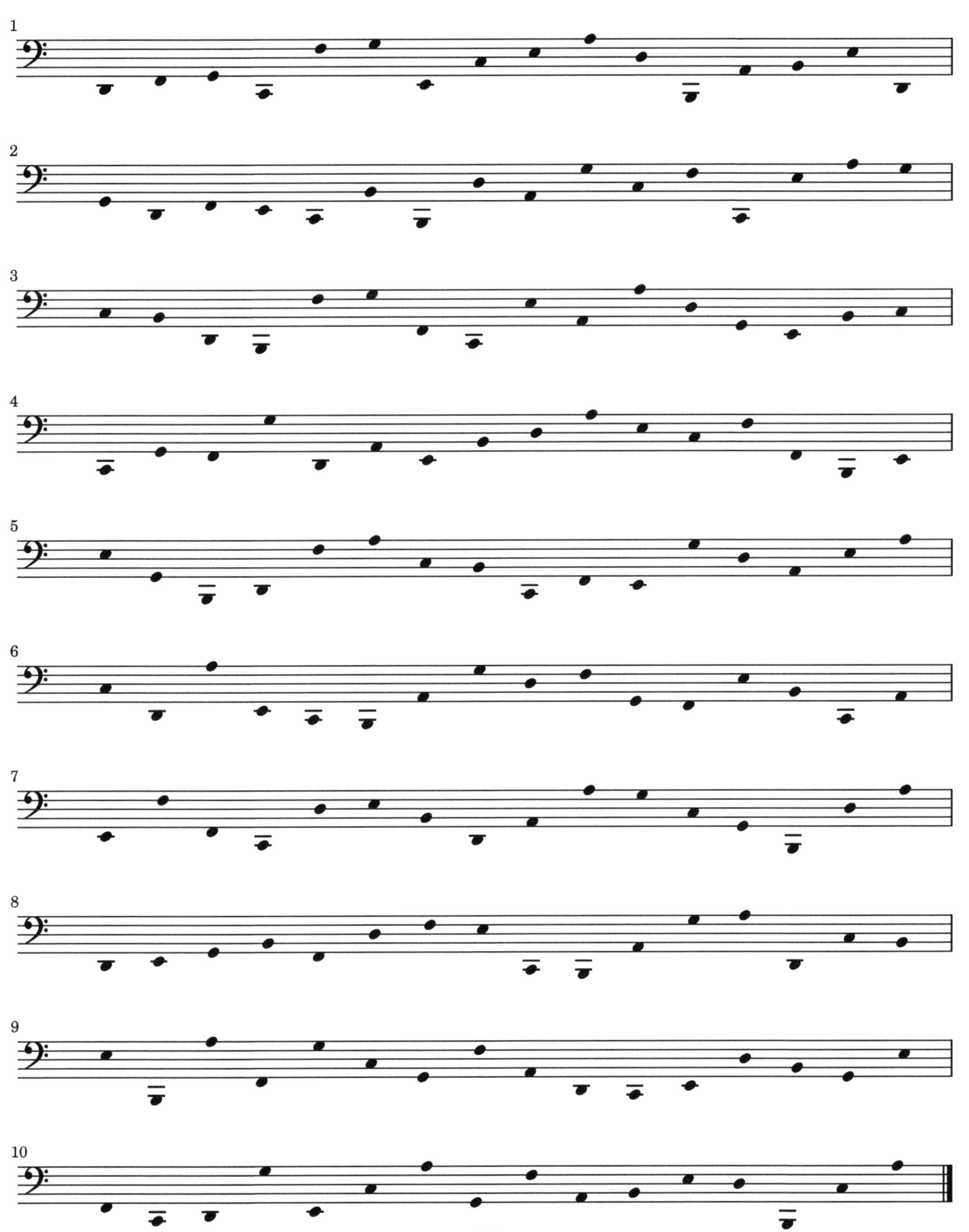

On and Below the Staff - Diatonic

Exercise 5 - Second Ledger Line

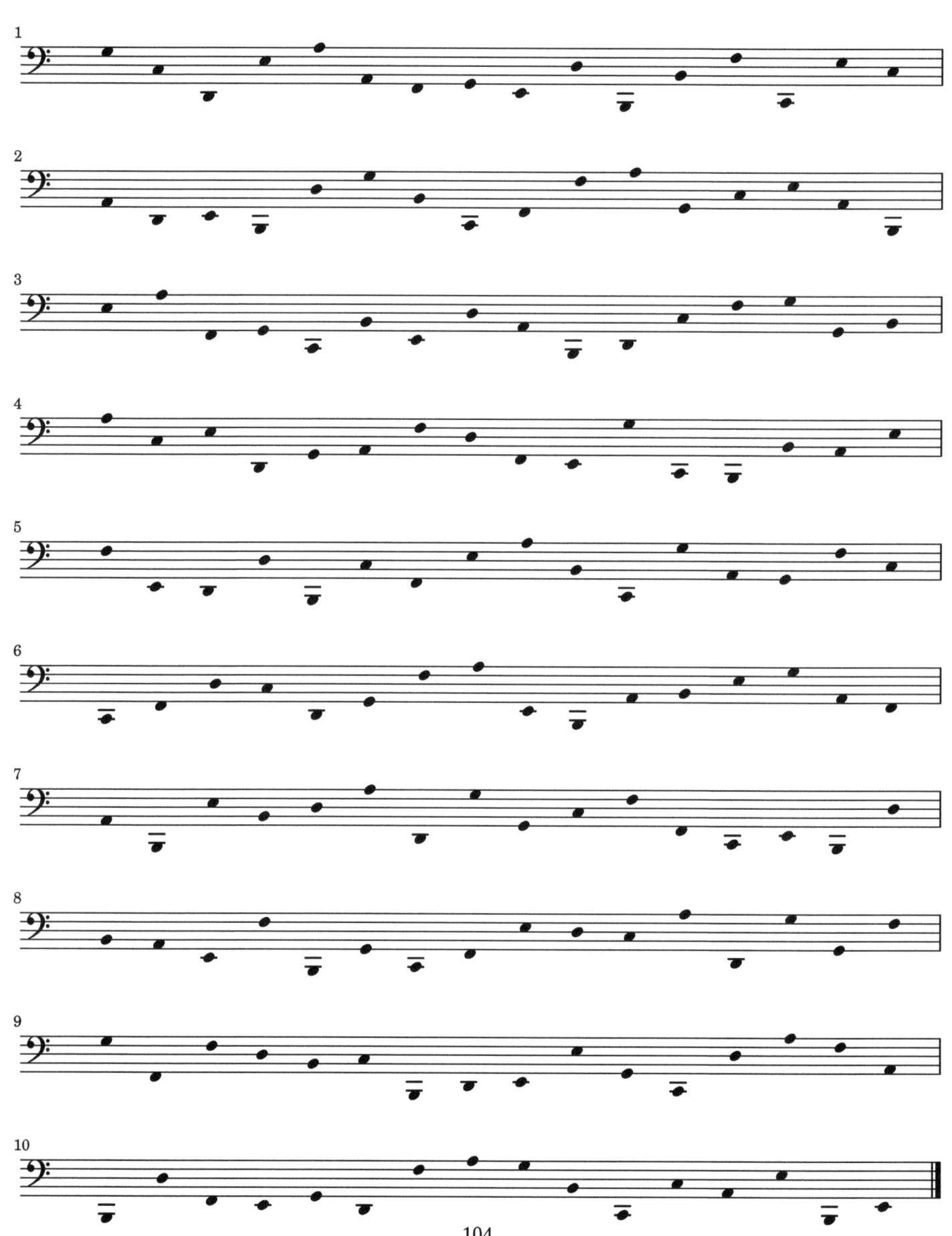

On and Below the Staff - Diatonic
Exercise 6 - Second Ledger Line

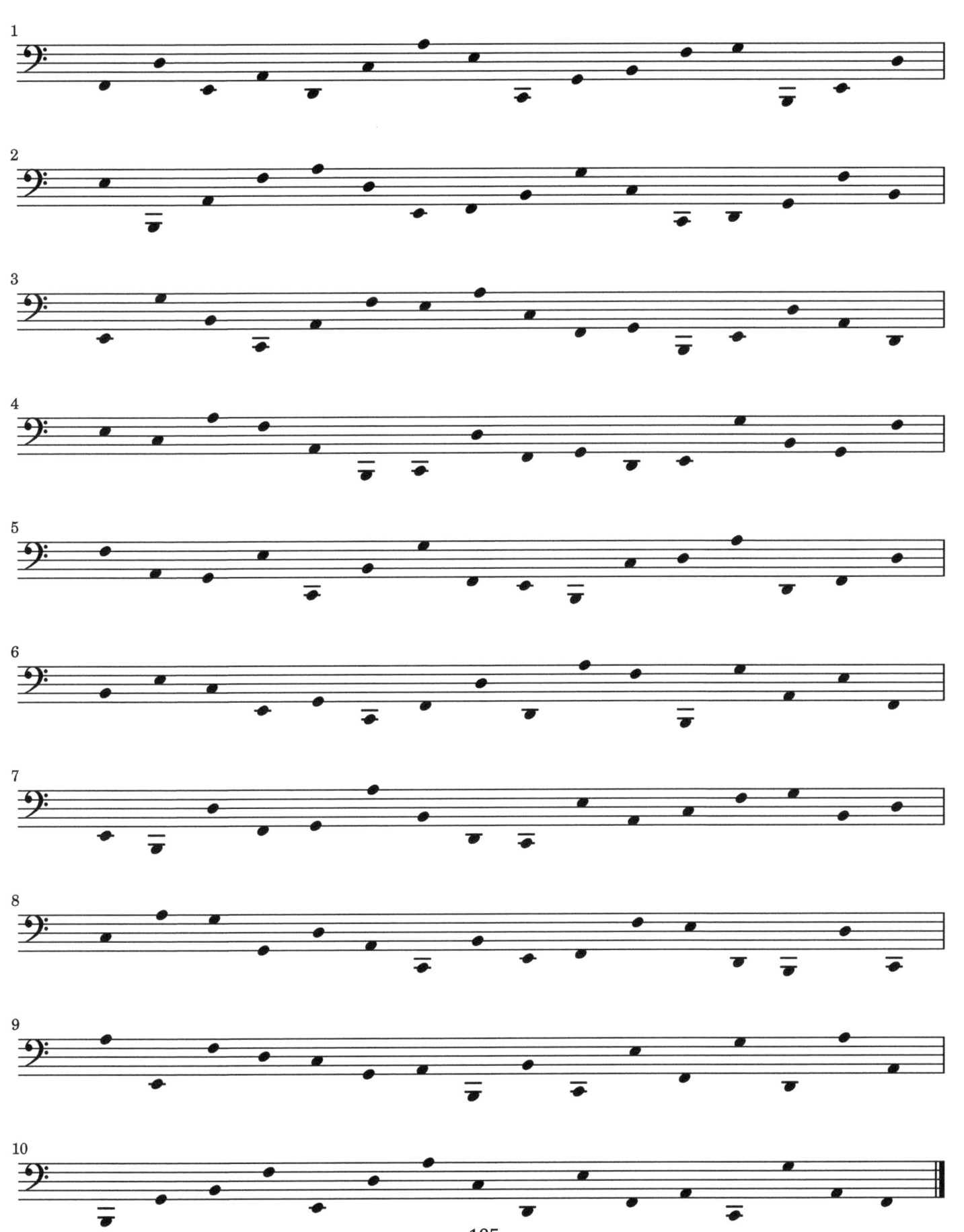

On and Below the Staff - Diatonic
Exercise 8 - Third Ledger Line

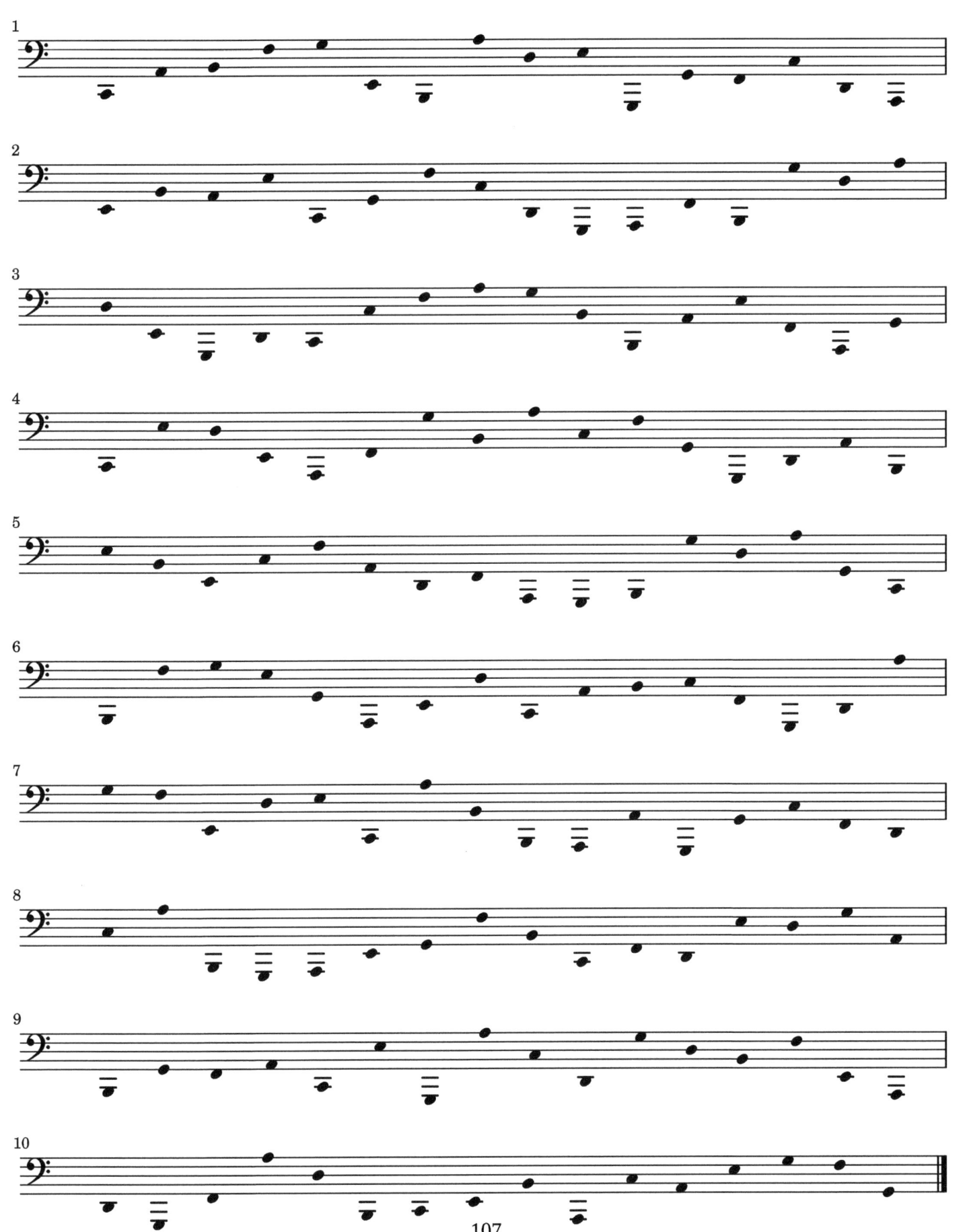

On and Below the Staff - Diatonic

Exercise 9 - Third Ledger Line

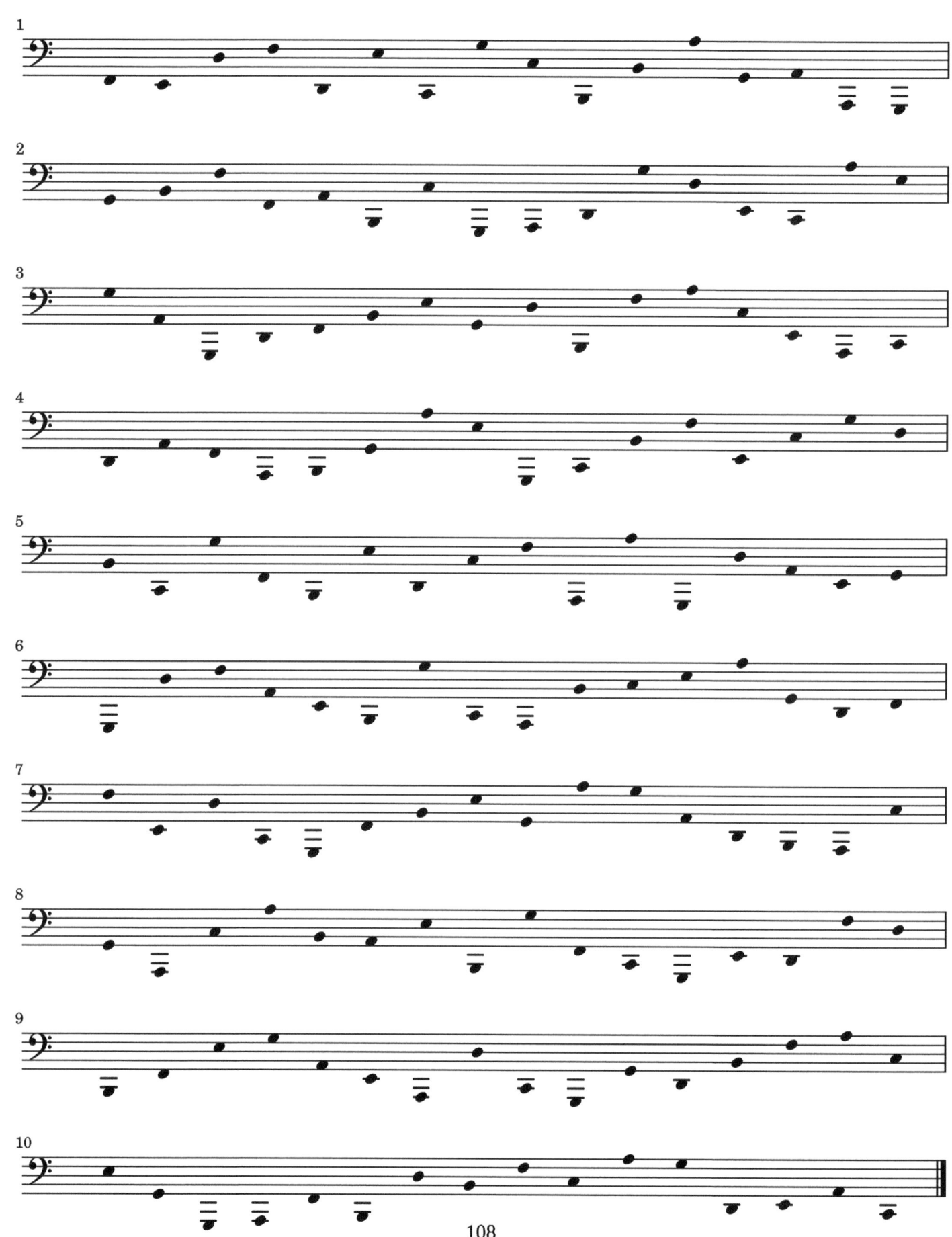

On and Below the Staff - Diatonic

Exercise 10 - Fourth Ledger Line

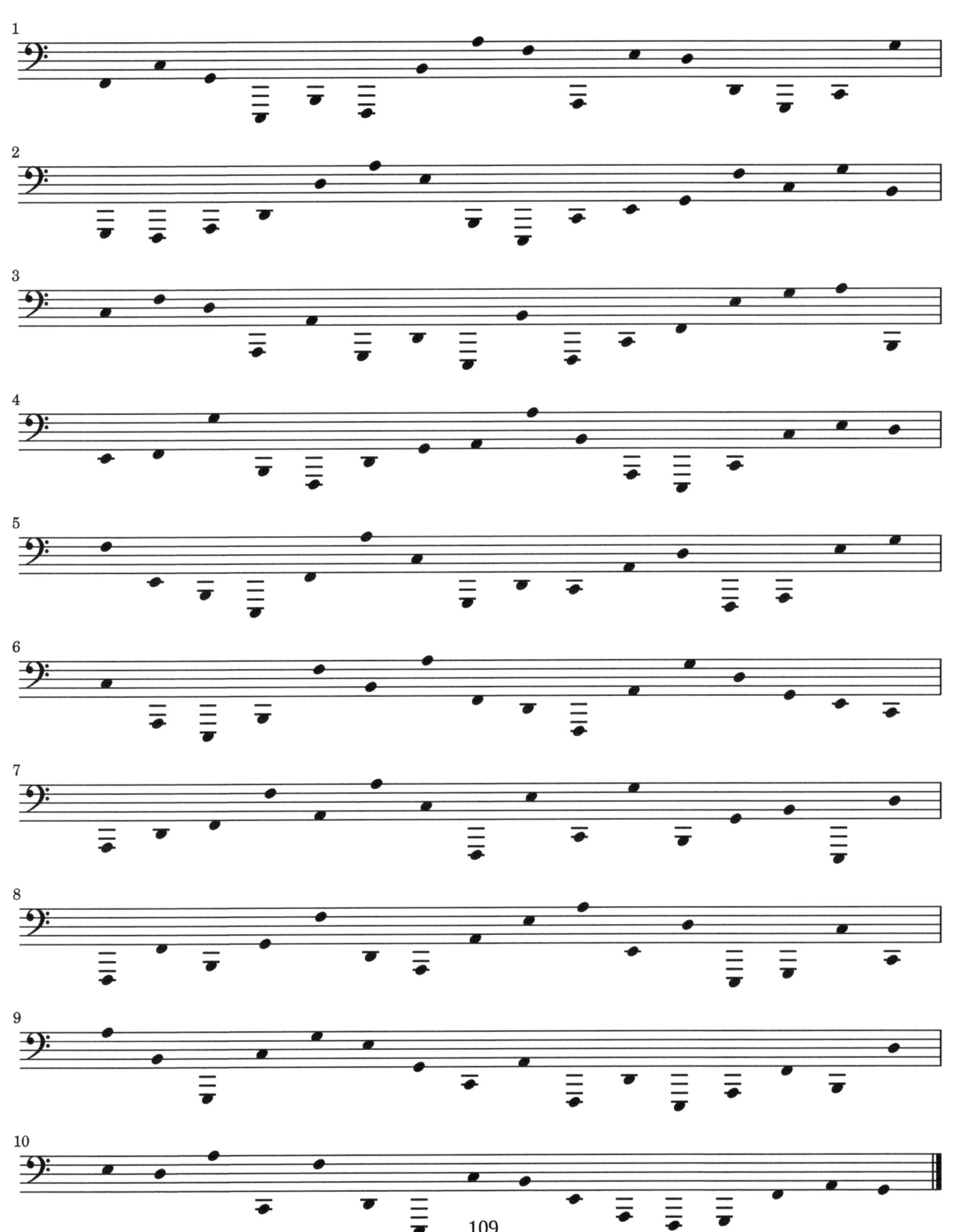

On and Below the Staff - Diatonic
Exercise 11 - Fourth Ledger Line

On and Below the Staff - Diatonic
Exercise 12 - Fourth Ledger Line

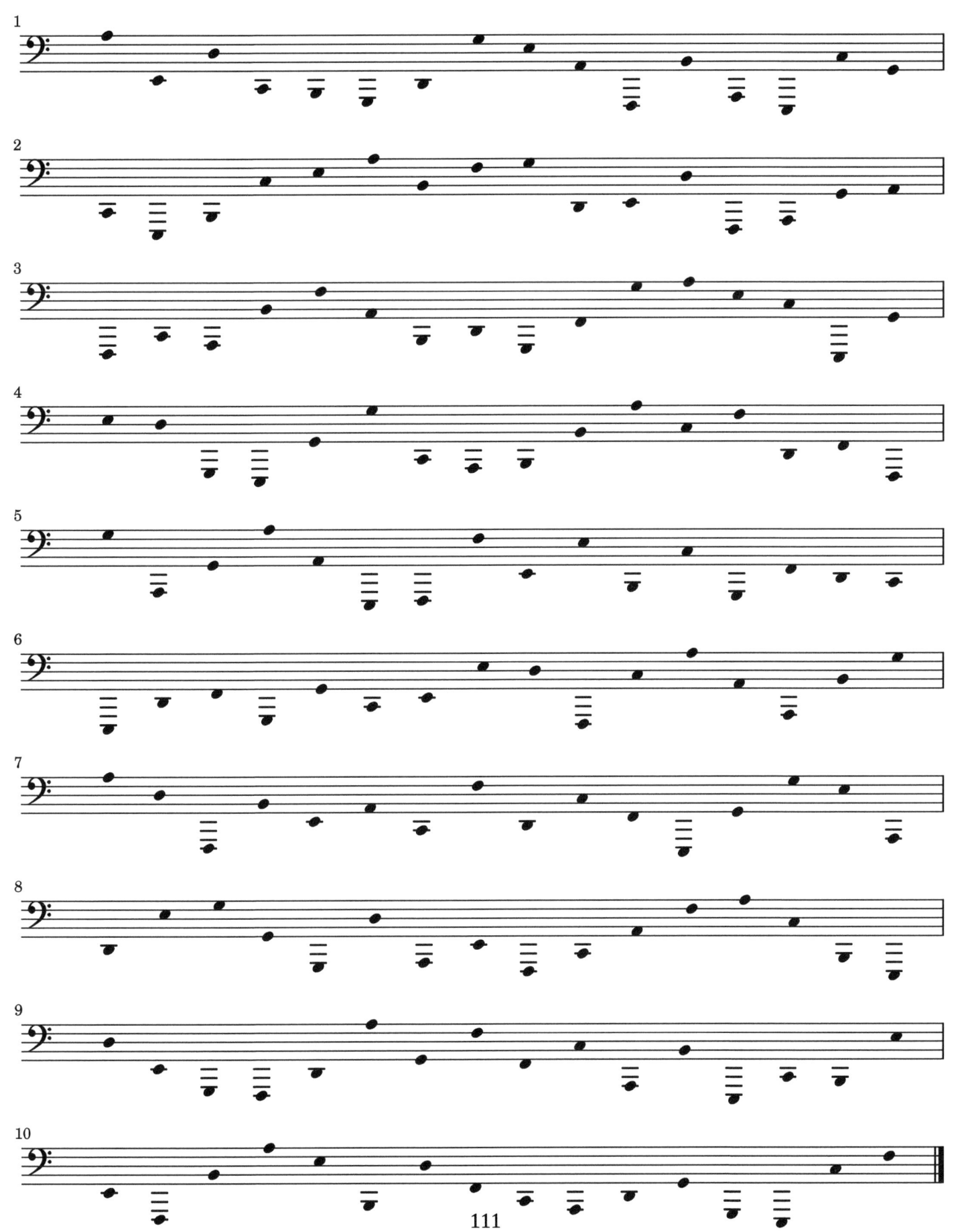

Chapter 10:

On and Below the Staff Chromatic

Exercise Ranges:

On and Below the Staff - Chromatic

Exercise 1 - First Ledger Line

On and Below the Staff - Chromatic
Exercise 2 - First Ledger Line

On and Below the Staff - Chromatic

Exercise 3 - First Ledger Line - Including B♯, C♭, E♯, F♭

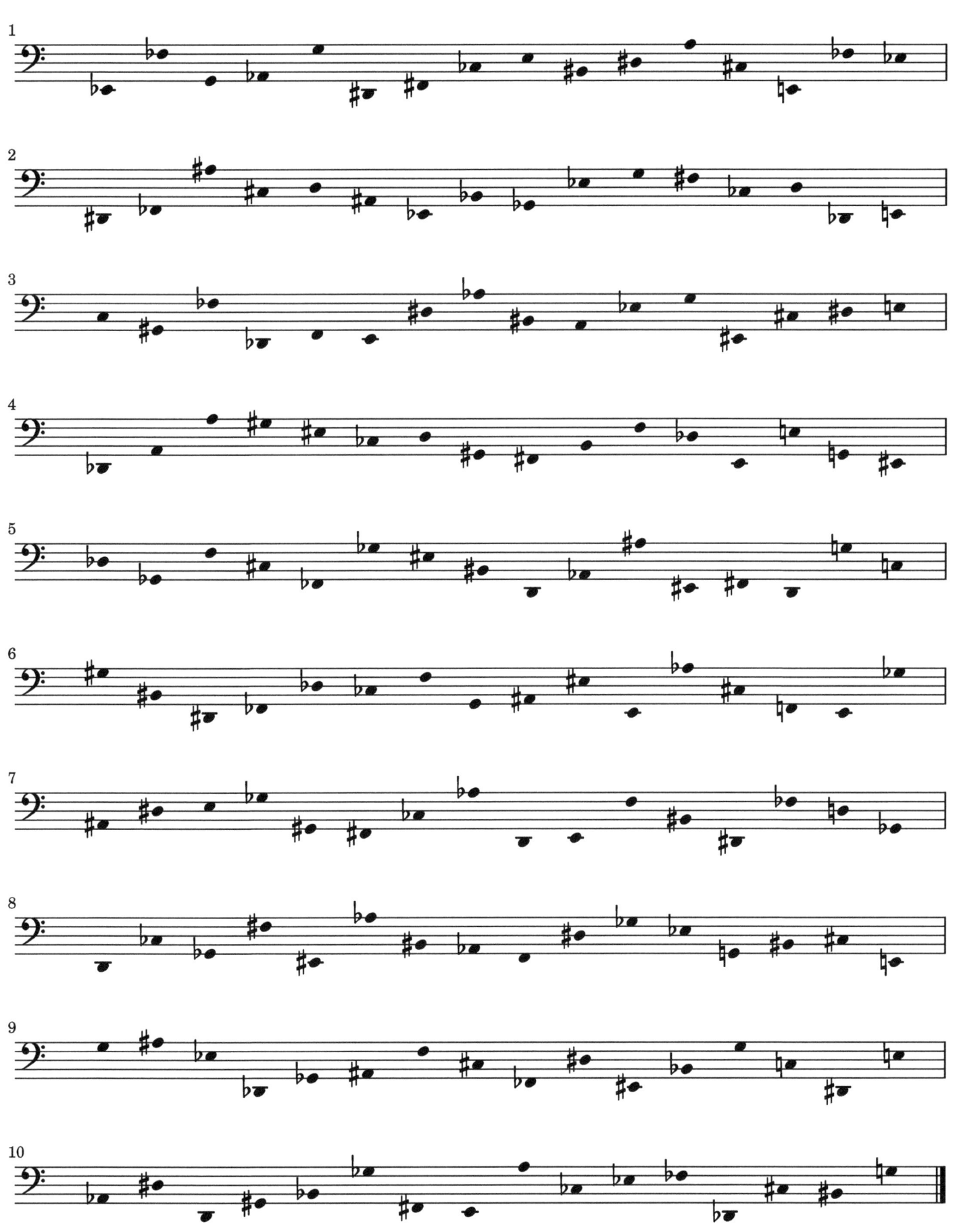

On and Below the Staff - Chromatic

Exercise 4 - Second Ledger Line

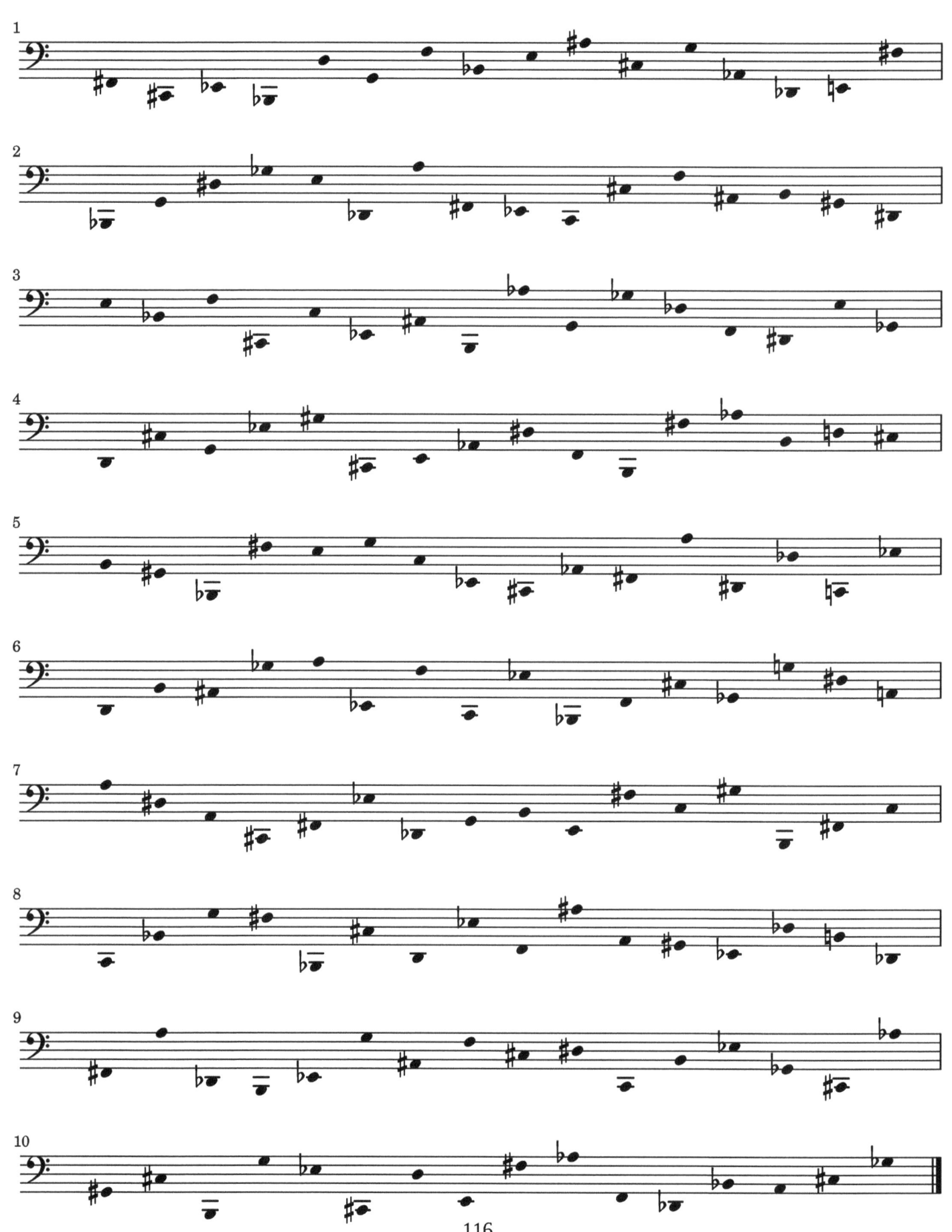

On and Below the Staff - Chromatic
Exercise 5 - Second Ledger Line

On and Below the Staff - Chromatic

Exercise 6 - Second Ledger Line - Including B♯, C♭, E♯, F♭

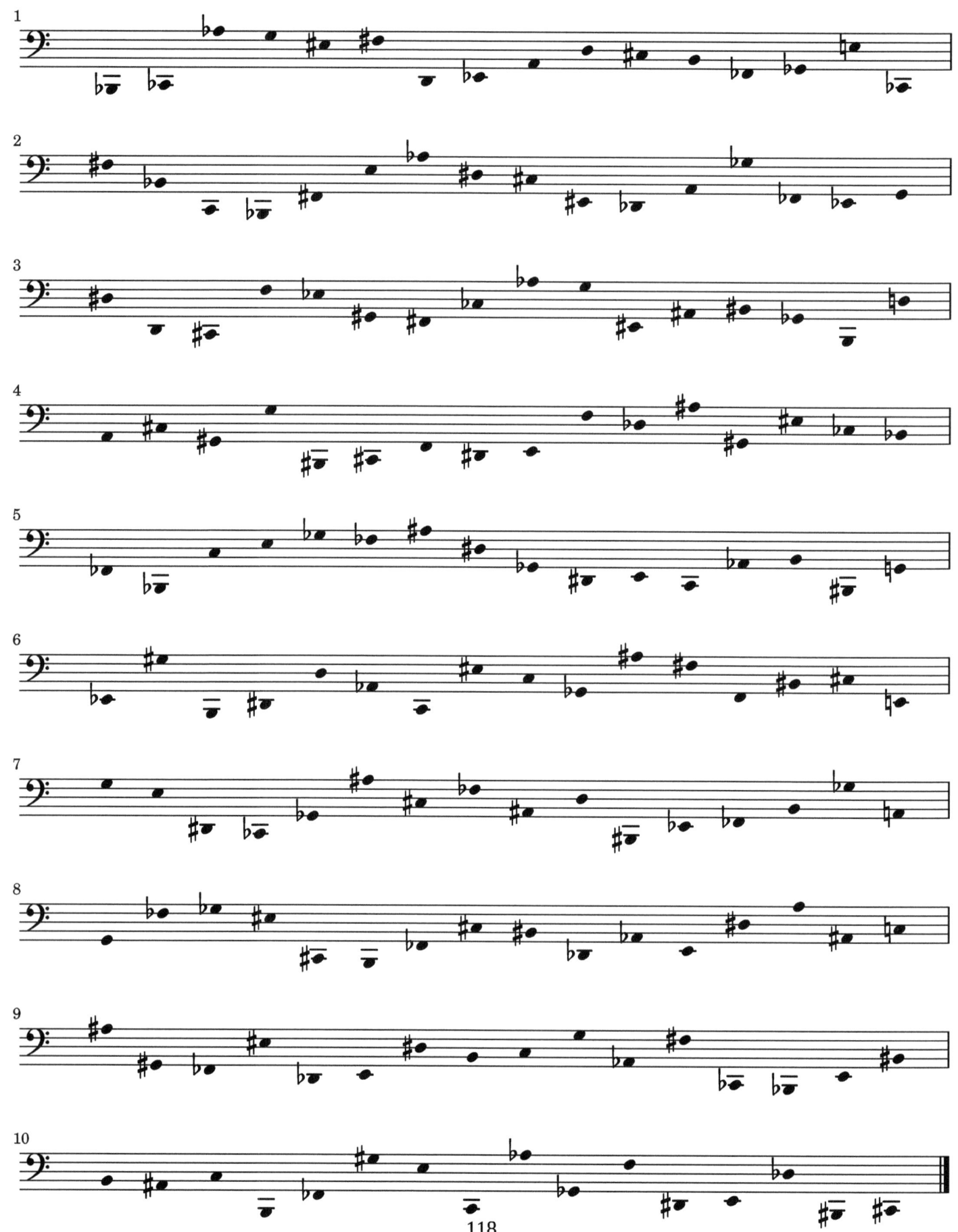

On and Below the Staff - Chromatic
Exercise 7 - Third Ledger Line

On and Below the Staff - Chromatic

Exercise 8 - Third Ledger Line

On and Below the Staff - Chromatic

Exercise 9 - Third Ledger Line - Including B#, C♭, E#, F♭

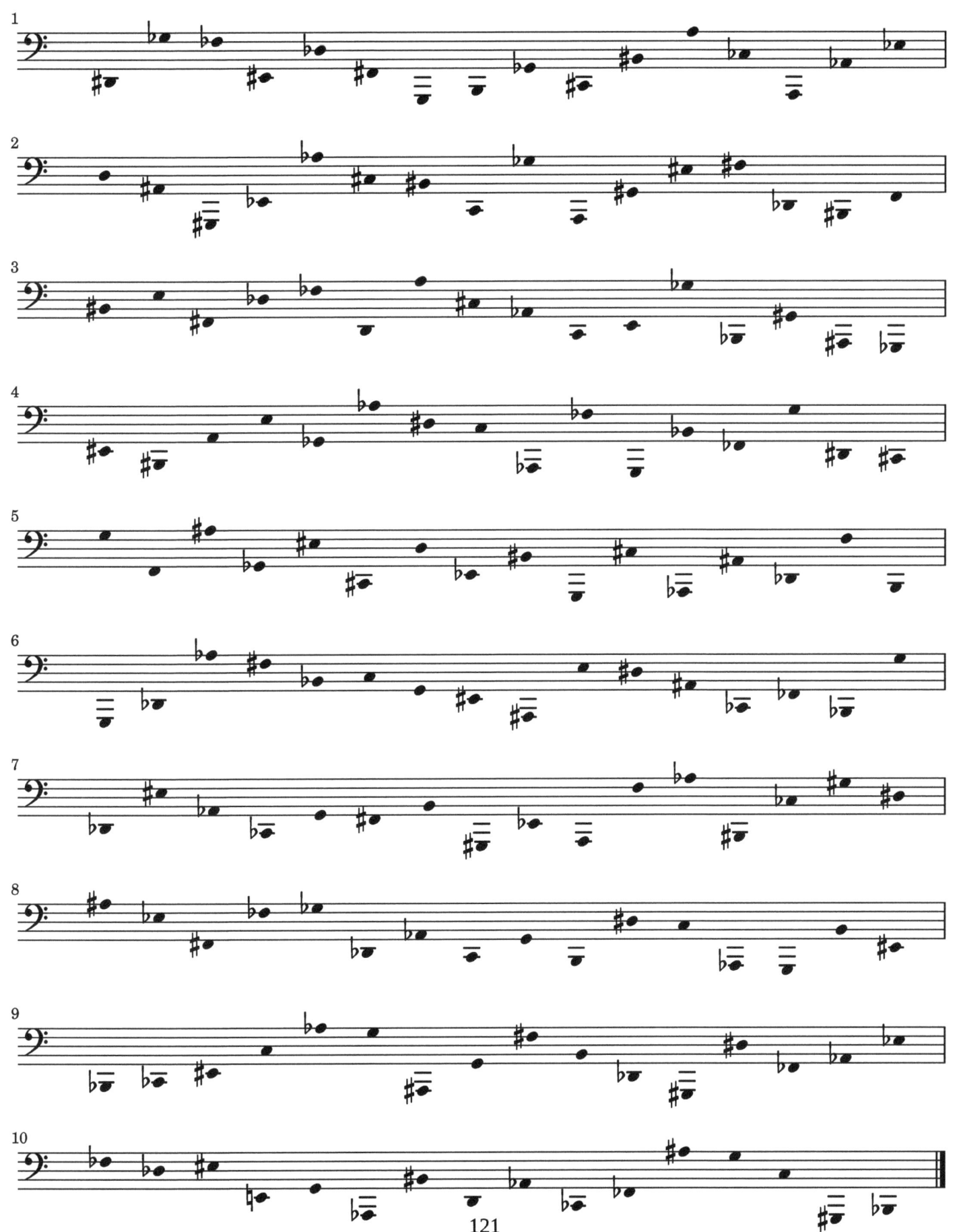

On and Below the Staff - Chromatic
Exercise 10 - Fourth Ledger Line

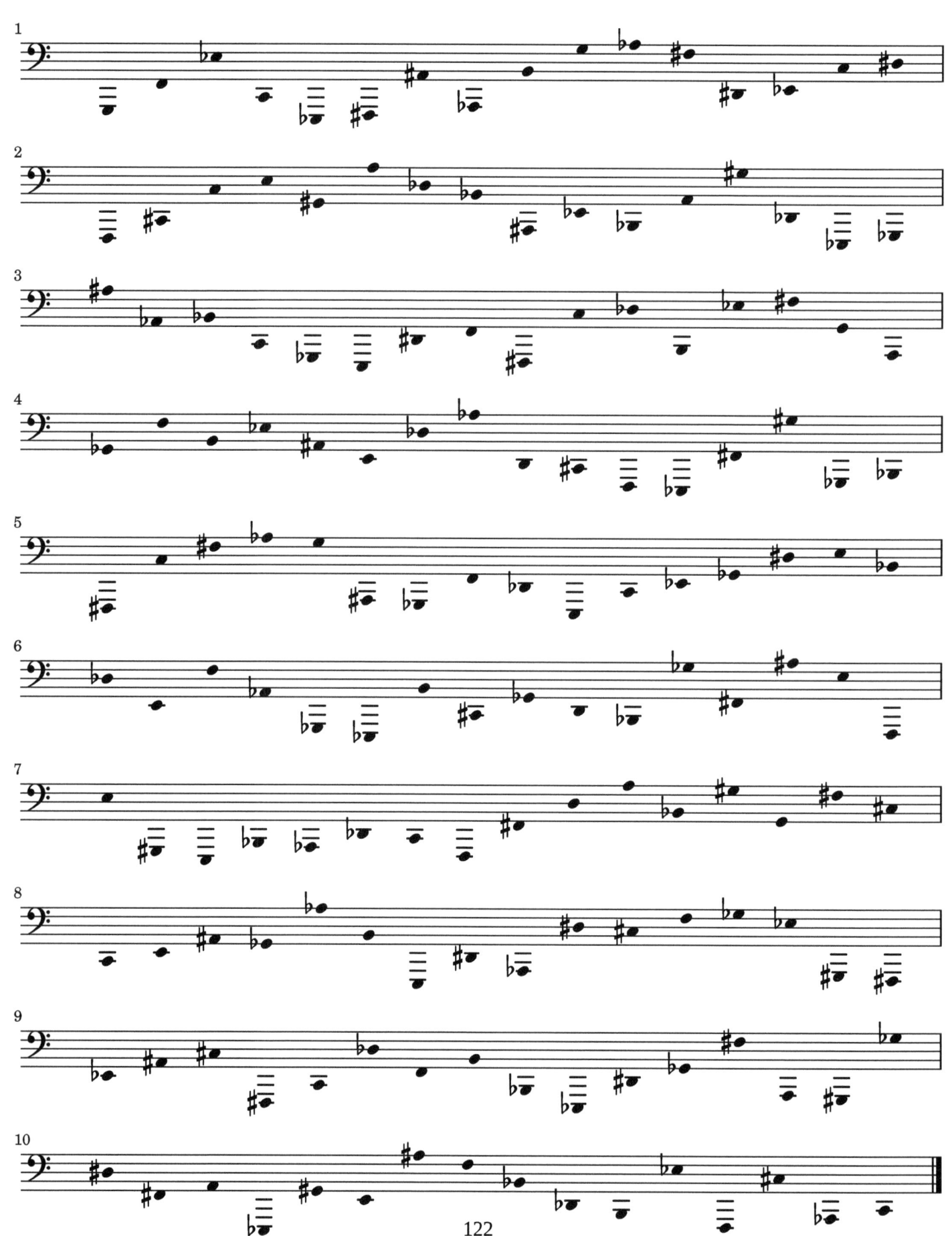

On and Below the Staff - Chromatic
Exercise 11 - Fourth Ledger Line

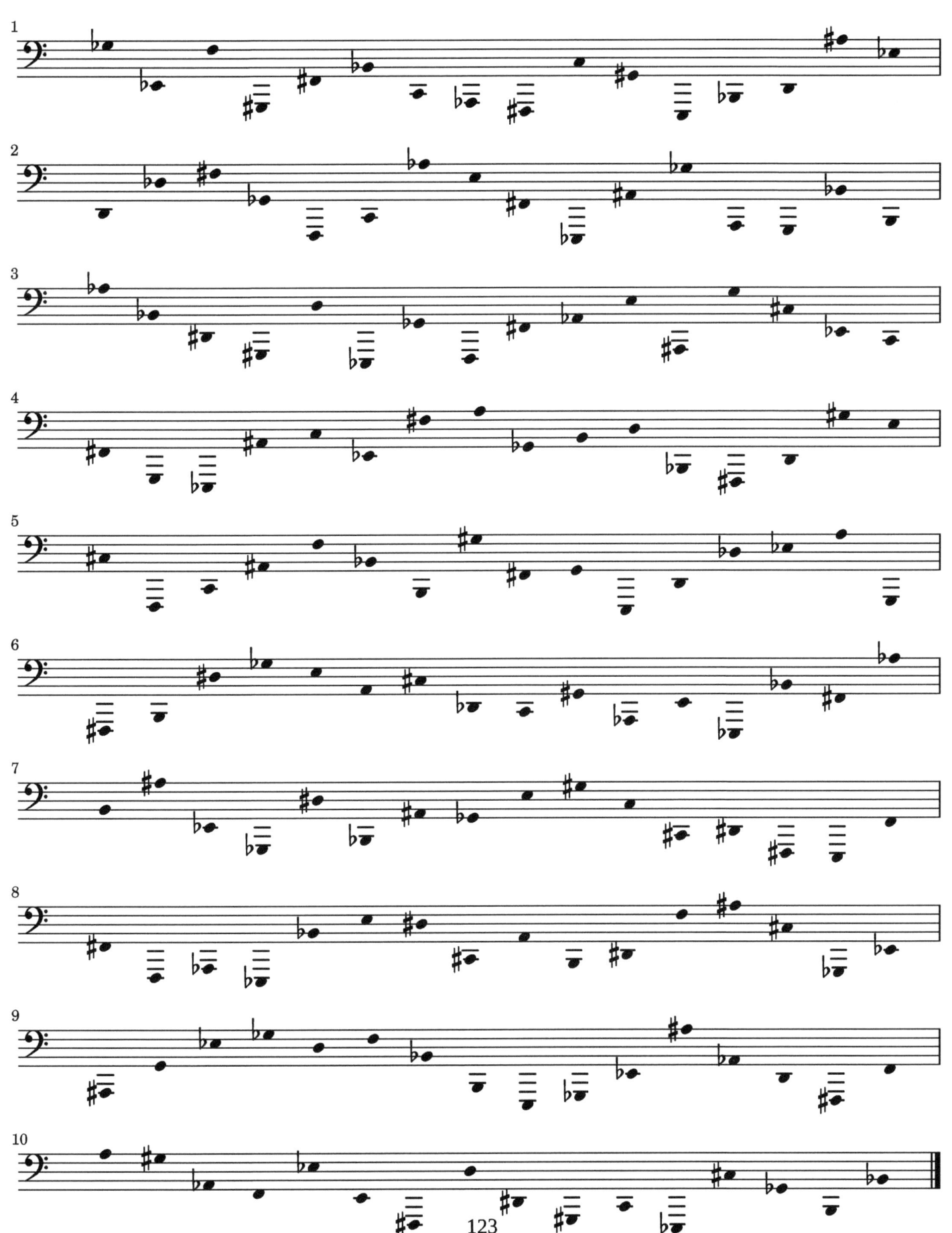

On and Below the Staff - Chromatic

Exercise 12 - Fourth Ledger Line - Including B♯, C♭, E♯, F♭

Thank You!

For more materials please visit
www.DotsandBeams.com

Milton Keynes UK
Ingram Content Group UK Ltd.
UKHW031441190324
439615UK00004B/118